D1313886

INSIDE THE DEMOCRATS' COVERED-UP CYBER SCANDAL

SPIES IN CONGRESS

FRANK MINITER

Post Hill
PRESS

A POST HILL PRESS BOOK

ISBN: 978-1-68261-803-5
ISBN (eBook): 978-1-68261-804-2

Spies in Congress
Inside the Democrats' Covered-Up Cyber Scandal
© 2018 by Frank Miniter
All Rights Reserved

Cover art by Christian Bentulan

Post Hill Press, LLC
New York • Nashville
posthillpress.com

Published in the United States of America

If liberty means anything at all,
it means the right to tell people what they
do not want to hear.

—*George Orwell*[1]

CONTENTS

THE DEMOCRATS' INTERNATIONAL SPY THRILLER

This at least cries out for a serious investigation, when you got people who have money problems hanging out with and getting a loan from someone who is known to hang out with Hezbollah and they have access to the server for dozens and dozens of Democrat officials in the United States Congress—I don't know, but that's a movie right there, I think.

—Rep. Jim Jordan (R-OH)[1]

Following the criminal trail of a group of former congressional employees as they are being investigated by Capitol Police and the Federal Bureau of Investigation offered a surreal gauntlet of surprises and obstacles. Capitol Police wouldn't answer even basic questions—partly, no doubt, because their oversight in this case failed miserably, but also because this is a spy scandal in the US House of Representatives most members of Congress would rather not admit exists.

For those surprised to see this referred to up front as a spy and criminal investigation with all the elements of a plot for a modern cyber thriller, as you'll see, the main actors in this story did spy on congressmen and their staffs. They copied congressmen's emails and more and even gave themselves access to official iPhones used by congressional staffers. According to an internal report by the House of Representatives' general (IG), their behavior mirrored a "classic method for insiders to exfiltrate data from an organization." They also continued to copy data to a server they had control of and then, when authorities were closing in, the entire server was physically stolen, according to a House Office of Inspector General report in September 2016.[2] This would be disputed by a plea-deal agreement in July 2018 by the Department of Justice. Whether they had sold the data they harvested from Congress still wasn't known as this was being written, at not least publicly, but no one has been able to give another plausible reason for why they were spying on congressmen.

Some former Central Intelligence Agency and FBI employees said it is important to see this as a spy story, as it checks all the boxes for how foreign intelligence services work. Also, looking at this team of Information Technology (IT) aides as only a criminal operation would mean investigators would only move to replace the locks and improve security, not to tackle the real threats to Congress and our democratic system such insider threats pose.

Some in the FBI and the Department of Justice (DOJ) were helpful, but personnel in those agencies and most congressional sources did insist on staying on background. The FBI turned down Freedom of Information Act (FOIA) requests, saying that the "FBI will neither confirm nor deny the existence of such records pursuant to FOIA exemptions...."

Few wanted their names mentioned in reporting about an ongoing case in which foreign-born and indicted congressional IT workers had, and perhaps still have, terabytes of emails and much more data on as many as forty-four congressmen. Some Democratic congressmen literally ran away when asked questions about this case in the halls of congressional buildings. Their favorite escape hatches were "members only" elevators. Some of these scenes were comic, as these weren't particularly young or fit people.

Even the Republican leadership in Congress was reluctant to go on the record—some sources say this is because bringing attention to this case would mean more light would also be shined on their congressional budgets, staffs, and power. Others pointed out that the Awans might still have plenty of dirt on congressmen and their staffs.

The subjects of this investigation were understandably reluctant to speak, but some of their associates, family members, and former tenants were very open. Many of the attorneys involved were also eager to get their names in print as they tried to shape the narrative. Congressional watchdog groups were very helpful as well, and some former US intelligence agency employees with decades of experience in the Middle East gave important context to what happened.

With these sources, court records, a lot of off-the-record interviews, and many on-the-record interviews, I set out to write a completely factual book that would stand on its own as a piece of journalism. If the people and events in this book at times seem too over the top to be real, please flip to the back of the book and review the endnotes and links to official documents. You'll see that everything is nailed down factually.

Though it is impossible to avoid what-ifs with such a complex and evolving case, especially one that many in power are actively trying to suppress, I declined to jump to conclusions about what some might have done, said, or felt. When you see something in quotes in these pages, it is because a source close to the investigation or to one of its participants spoke or wrote those words. I always tried to verify all accounts with others, but in some cases, this wasn't possible. When I couldn't, I tell you so.

What kept this thumping along was that, like a Russian *matryoshka* doll, every development in this true story resulted in deeper problems waiting with contemptuous smiles—and, as you'll see, many of these modern problems can and likely will affect every American and our freedom in profound ways.

Actually, it is as if Rep. Debbie Wasserman Schultz (D-FL) set out to purposely give us the most outlandish villains at her disposal, people who could expose her and the Democratic National Committee (DNC) to everything in their cluttered closets, so that we could, by piecing the story together, see through the looking glass right into the DNC's political alternate reality.

As the picture comes into focus, you can't help notice that what happened to Hillary Clinton's presidential ambitions—as well as all that was behind the leaks that rocked the DNC in the 2016 presidential election cycle, and even, more recently, the reasons behind Representative Wasserman Schultz's downfall—might all be explained by the curious, exploding, yet at the same time hushed-up investigation into Imran Awan and his overpaid band of accomplices.

If you were to meet Imran Awan, Wasserman Schultz's former IT aide, you might think that an overstatement, as at first glance Imran hardly seems like a Hollywood villain central casting would find very compelling.

Imran is of average height and looks for a middle-aged man from Pakistan. He is lean and still has his short-trimmed dark hair as he nears forty. He wore sharp, fashionable suits and shiny leather shoes to his court appearances and would leave, without talking to media, with a fast stride making his heels click on the Washington sidewalk. Calling him *GQ* might be too far, but he fits seamlessly in the scene as an urban professional in our nation's capital.

When asked about Imran, many said he is a secretive sort of guy, though a few congressional aides confided that he "creeped them out" when he told them what he could have the police do to people back in Pakistan. One said, "Imran was always elusive and didn't talk much to other IT aides. Still, there was just something slimy about him."

Someone could, of course, say the same thing about some congressmen. But one IT aide who has worked for members of Congress for more than a decade said it was very strange that Imran, while Representative Wasserman Schultz ran the DNC, always seemed to be at all the hip parties. "IT aides aren't typically invited to White House affairs and other high-profile political events," he said. "We're mostly in the background. But I'd hear that Imran was going to some of those Washington shindigs."

There is a widely published photo of Imran with former president Bill Clinton from one of these affairs. Imran is leaning in as Bill stands straight and looks forward. Behind them is a long blue curtain. They are at a political event during the 2016 election cycle, and Imran was obviously trying to sneak into a photo with the ex-president as Bill looked with his politician's smile into flashing cameras.

Imran is from Faisalabad, Pakistan's third-largest city. It has a population of about 3.4 million and is so cosmopolitan it has been called the "Manchester of Pakistan." When he was fourteen years old, Imran applied for a US visa in a lottery established by the Immigration Act of 1990. He applied through the US Embassy in Pakistan for what is called a "Diversity Visa," a program that grants 55,000 immigrant visas each fiscal year.

As this was being written, the Immigration Act of 1990 was the last big change in now very controversial US immigration law, and what a change it was. It was first introduced by Sen. Ted Kennedy in 1989 and was signed into law by George H. W. Bush. It increased total immigration figures to allow 675,000 immigrants into the United States per year after 1994. It provided family-based immigration visas (which is how Imran's brothers, father, and others in his circle came to America), created five distinct employment-based visas, and began the Diversity Immigrant Visa Program Imran used to get into the country.

Regarding the latter, the US Embassy in Pakistan says on its website: "The lottery aims to diversify the immigrant population in the United States, by selecting applicants mostly from countries with low rates of immigration to the United States in the previous five years."

Imran arrived in the United States at just seventeen years old determined to be an American success story. He certainly became adept at understanding the American system—its strengths, biases, and especially its oversights and flaws. Alexis de Tocqueville would have been impressed with how quickly Imran came to understand the American liberal mind of the early twenty-first century.

His first job, like the children of so many working-class Americans, was at a fast-food restaurant. He also soon enrolled in a community college in northern Virginia. The *Washington Post* reported that he later "transferred to Johns Hopkins University in Baltimore and earned a degree in information technology."[3] The National Student

Clearinghouse did confirm that Imran graduated with a Bachelor of Science in information systems from Johns Hopkins in 2004.

Imran also became a naturalized U.S. citizen in 2004. In this same year he was hired for a part-time job as an IT specialist in the office of Rep. Robert Wexler (D-FL). He did well socially in the prim offices with the typically young and well-educated people who make up our representatives' staffs in the congressional buildings.

Imran can be charismatic and likeable—many said this, and his two wives (he allegedly secretly married another in Pakistan, even though he was not divorced from the first) can probably attest to it, too. He used this skill to get to know some of Wexler's staffers as he worked for a company that provided services to Wexler's office.

Wexler left Congress in 2010 and is now president of the Washington-based S. Daniel Abraham Center for Middle East Peace, a nonprofit advocacy group that works with leaders and policymakers in the United States and the Middle East "to help reach a just and comprehensive peace that will bring an end to the Arab–Israeli conflict."

But Imran was in, and he prospered.

Long before Wexler left office, Imran began working in many other Democrats' offices. As an IT specialist, he set up printers and email accounts for new employees and did other computer-related work. "Charismatic and accommodating, he became a popular choice among House Democrats and soon cobbled together more than a dozen part-time jobs as what is known as a 'shared employee' on the Hill, floating between offices on an as-needed basis," said the *Washington Post*.

That is the fluffy American-success-story stuff the *Washington Post* reported in a nothing-to-see-here exposé. But there is a lot more to Imran, his associates, and everything they got into. Imran in particular is worth following, seedy as you'll soon find him to be, because what he really represents is a fissure going right to the heart of our political system. This is because an IT person can see everything, especially one like Imran, a greedy person who copied everything to a server he controlled and to a private Dropbox account—and everything in this case means the emails, meeting schedules, and more for as many as forty-four Democratic congressmen that he or his team worked for.

Perhaps that Imran had (and maybe still has) all of this personal data on elected officials—we don't know if he'd also gotten ahold of the DNC's secrets, as he was working for Representative Wasserman Schultz while she ran the DNC—might explain why the Democrats who hired Imran and his wife, brothers, and others (some as what Rep. Louie Gohmert called "ghost employees")[4] aren't so keen to talk about him. This just might be why Wasserman Schultz has aggressively accused anyone who asks about this case of being guilty of "ethnic and religious profiling."[5]

Actually, to push this religious-profiling angle, the law firm representing Imran Awan (Gowen Rhoades Winograd & Silva PLLC) published several statements attacking the messengers (the few journalists writing about this). One statement said, "The attacks on Mr. Awan and his family began as part of a frenzy of anti-Muslim bigotry in the literal heart of our democracy, the House of Representatives. For months we have had utterly unsupported, outlandish, and slanderous statements targeting Mr. Awan coming not just from the ultra-right-wing 'pizzagate' media but from sitting members of Congress. Now we have the Justice Department showing up with a complaint about disclosures on a modest real estate matter. To an extent, the situation speaks for itself."[6]

This statement also said that Imran's "family is presently staying with extended family in Pakistan because he and his wife were both abruptly and unjustly fired, leaving them without a reliable source of income to pay typical US living expenses, and because extremist right-wing bloggers were beginning to harass them and their children—even going to their children's schools. Mr. Awan has stayed in the United States to earn some income to manage this situation as best as possible. He attempted to travel this week to see his family for the first time in months. The government had been informed he would travel and had stated no objection. Yet on Monday night he was hastily arrested at Dulles airport."

So Imran's lawyers quickly cast him as a victim of "extremist right-wing bloggers" and anti-Muslim bigots.

Rep. Debbie Wasserman Schultz, meanwhile, responded to media requests with this statement: "After details of the investigation were reviewed with us, my office was provided no evidence to indicate that laws had been broken, which over time, raised troubling concerns about due process, fair treatment and potential ethnic and religious profiling. Upon learning of his arrest, he was terminated."

No matter that it took Representative Wasserman Schultz from February 2, 2017, (the date Imran and his associates were booted off the congressional computer system) to the end of July 2017, (when he was arrested trying to leave the country) for her to finally fire Imran.

Ironically, as Wasserman Schultz characterized those looking into this case as bigots, every part of this story was fueled not just by Imran Awan and his many schemes, but because of ideological blinders the DNC purposely fashioned for itself as it played its brand of identity politics.

Along the way you'll see that political theater like this is amusing and enlightening, sure, but what's really important is what this mad tale exposes. There is a new digital reality, and members of Congress, as they are finding out, can't exempt themselves from its consequences. To keep and even regain our freedom, we must understand what this case has to teach the rest of us as well.

CHAPTER 1

CHEATS IN THE BIG GAME

IT Guys: A group of men who are above gossip, are extremely friendly, and most likely are hung like horses.

Tammy: "Just to get back at those guys, we are going to call them the It Guys!"

Group of guys: "Well, thanks for the compliment!"

—Urban Dictionary[1]

Capitol Police watched Imran Awan, his wife, brothers, and other team members for at least six months before they took action on February 2, 2017. Somewhere along the way, Capitol Police began getting assistance from the FBI's Joint Terrorism Task Force, specialized units that "provide one-stop shopping for information regarding terrorist activities,"[2] according to the FBI. As they waited and watched, Imran Awan and his crew did odd and alarming things on the computer network used by members of Congress and their staffs.

Capitol Police waited to act even though Imran often traveled, sometimes for months at a time, to Pakistan. They waited despite that Imran sometimes, according to sources close to the investigation, worked remotely by logging on to Congress's system from Pakistan.[3]

When asked how logging in to Congress's network from abroad might be possible, an IT aide who has worked for members of Congress for more than a decade said, "If you have the passwords and internet access, you can log in to the congressional system from anywhere. Congressional staffers often travel, even internationally, so there is often justification for logging on remotely. Still, Imran's behavior should have drawn attention."

Investigators found that, over time, Imran grew his team of congressional IT contractors as he made more connections in Congress and as each new member of his team reached a salary cap. (Basically, congressional staffers, including contractors, can't make more than the average congressman's annual salary of $174,000.

Imran had started working in congressional offices in 2004. He brought his brother Abid on as an IT specialist in 2005. His wife, Hina Alvi, got her first job as an IT administrator for a congressman's office in 2007. Imran's friend Rao Abbas, who had previously worked as a manager at a McDonald's, started in 2012. And Imran's youngest brother, Jamal, got a high-paying gig working in congressional offices in 2014. Each would hold part-time jobs in multiple Democratic congressional offices. Well, some of them likely didn't really work for members of Congress—all we do know, according to official records, is they were paid to work for members of Congress. Jamal was actually a full-time student during much of this time, and Abid ran a car dealership that would go bankrupt in 2012. Yet they were both paid for full-time work by Congress.

Imran's first job with Congress was as a part-time IT specialist in the office of Rep. Robert Wexler (D-FL). Imran was then a contractor working for InterAmerica, a company now known as iConstituent. The firm was established in 2002 and, as of late 2017, was one of six firms on an approved list of IT contractors given to congressmen so they can hire people from vetted companies. Actually, that there are only six firms, many of them small, on this list shocked other IT professionals who were interviewed as background for this book. "With all the IT firms in the area, only six are on their list?" said one.

Obviously, the IT professionals said, Congress put little thought into IT support even though IT aides have access to private records of many members of Congress.

The US Senate is run differently. Senate offices typically have a full-time IT administrator on staff. The reason is that Senate staffs are often larger than House staffs and, as they represent entire states, they tend to have more field offices back in the senator's home state, offices that might each employ a dozen or more people.

Most of the 435 members of the House of Representatives, however, don't require that much technical support. They typically hire IT professionals from the list of approved companies as they need them and often use these people as "shared" employees with other congressional offices.

Until late 2017, these approved contractors were held to a much higher standard than individual contractors. "Independent contractors basically didn't go through any background check," said an IT aide who has worked in the House for over a decade. "Since I started working on the Hill, however, companies have always had to go through background checks. Those who run the company and the IT aides they place in Congress all get fingerprinted, are interviewed, and so on."

In the fall of 2017, he said, "the House started to implement better security protocols. It was like they were suddenly going step-by-step to put in place Microsoft's recommended security criteria."

Imran Awan did work for an approved contractor when he started, so presumably there was a background check done on him at that time (Capitol Police would not confirm this), but he soon managed to cut the contractor (his middleman) out of the deal and was hired as an independent contractor. Later, he managed to bring his friends and family members in, even though they never worked for an approved contractor and most of them didn't have any IT training.

Congressmen are allowed to hire contractors on their own. The official *Members' Congressional Handbook* says:

> Members may contract with firms or individuals
> only for general (outside core office functions),

non-legislative and non-financial, office services (e.g., equipment maintenance, information technology services, data entry, staff training, photography, custodial services, web services, personal security contractors) for a specified time period not to exceed the Member's current term. Such contracts are reimbursable. Such contractors are not employees of the House and are ineligible for government-provided personnel benefits.

Contractors do not count against the Member's employee ceiling.

Members are advised to consult the Committee on House Administration before entering into such contracts. The Committee has set standards for many technology contracts in the Services section of the Guide to Outfitting an Office.[4]

Still, if Capitol Police had done background checks on the family and friends Imran brought in as independent contractors—all of whom had access to congressmen's personal emails and other sensitive data—they haven't said so.

The rules have recently been changed to prevent this oversight, according to Rep. Louie Gohmert (R-TX),[5] but in the next breath he asked, "But was there a background ever done on Imran Awan?"

Gohmert had earlier said on the floor of Congress:

I am told by...IT professionals that do work [in Congress] that, if you know what you are doing and you have access to even one Congress member's computer, which means their calendar, their emails, and notes taken and stored on the computer about meetings, then it is very easy—[if] you are good—to access virtually anybody else's information here in Congress. I was told some time back by one of my friends in intelligence that at one time there was concern about positions I had taken like in support of Egypt against the Muslim Brotherhood and that there were those who were monitoring people that came to my office. I was told that they know everybody that walks into your office. So when you see these kinds of reports, Mr. Speaker, it is a little disconcerting. It is disconcerting that people are not more concerned here in this body about the potential for the kind of breach that is being stated here.[6]

"Disconcerting" isn't a strong enough word for the situation Imran Awan and his team placed certain members of Congress in. Imran and his crew had access to all the emails, incoming and outgoing, and the computer files of the members of Congress they worked for. Over time, these congressmen included three members of the House Intelligence Committee and five members of the House Foreign Affairs Committee.

Incredibly, according to Representative Gohmert, it was unclear even to members of Congress what kind of background checks Capitol Police perform on IT contractors before they are allowed to work for Congress. Capitol Police also wouldn't go on the record to explain how they protect our congressmen. The FBI did reply to a request for information. Kelsey Pietranton, a spokesperson for the FBI, said the agency doesn't do any vetting of IT professionals for Congress.[7]

Though Capitol Police declined to respond to questions about its vetting process for IT professionals, the fact that some have slipped through without any scrutiny is hardly an unknown or new problem.

On May 21, 2008, the House inspector general, James J. Cornell, testified before the Committee on House Administration and said there was "inadequate oversight"[8] over shared employees like Imran Awan and his associates. Nevertheless, Capitol Police and Congress let Imran continue to grow his band of accomplices right under their noses for over a decade. In that time, Imran and his team of unvetted "IT professionals" were paid over four million dollars courtesy of American taxpayers.

Back in 2008, Inspector General Cornell said, "In most instances, [independent contractors] have all the freedom of a vendor and all the benefits of an employee without the accountability one would expect with an employee." At the time, he said IT specialists "present an additional risk in that they often have access to multiple offices' data outside of both the oversight of congressional office staff and the visibility of House security personnel."⁹

This had come up in 2008 after an employee of the House of Representatives was caught in an embezzlement scheme. Rep. Robert A. Brady (D-PA), then chairman of the Committee on House Administration, said in that 2008 hearing:

> During the transition between the 109th and 110th Congress, the House inspector general was conducting a routine audit. He was looking at the House system for uncovering and limiting duplicate payments. His investigators found the troubling record of embezzlement by one employee of the House. An employee defrauded the House of more than $160,000, a crime that was made easier by the fact that the employee was employed by several different congressional offices, and none of them knew the duplicate charges were made by the others. The IG brought the findings of embezzlement to our committee on February 2, 2007. The criminal procedure against that one employee took its course. But we then asked the IG to conduct a further review—how did the system of shared employees make congressional offices vulnerable to waste, misuse of data, or even outright theft, and what could we do about it?

House Inspector General Cornell then told the congressmen in attendance:

> Recently, we identified fifty-one shared employees that were on the payroll of at least three and up

to fourteen offices each. Their availability allows congressional offices to meet their support needs without having to hire full-time personnel with requisite skills and experience. However, through our audit and investigative work, we have found three major areas where the current controls over the practices of shared employees are either unenforced or weak and in need of significant improvement. If not addressed, these control weaknesses place congressional offices at significant risk of illegal or other improper activity occurring within their financial and administrative functions.

The first of the three areas of control weakness with shared employees is inadequate oversight over their activities. In most instances, they have all the freedom of a vendor and all the benefits of an employee without the accountability one would expect with an employee. Current practices do not provide for other office staff to review their day-to-day work, ensure they attend appropriate training, or stay current on House policies and procedures. Congressional offices may know their shared employee works for other offices, but they do not know how many or which ones.

Therefore, they cannot determine if there are conflicts of interest within the functions performed or with the other offices served. We identified seven financial shared employees that were employed by ten or more offices and eight IT shared employees that were serving as system administrators for eleven or more offices. In both disciplines, a few serve both majority and minority offices simultaneously. Under current practices, the work schedules of shared employees are also not monitored. Most of them are paid a flat monthly fee by the offices regardless of their time and effort expended. IT shared employees with administrator rights present an additional risk in that they often have access to multiple offices' data outside of both the oversight of congressional office staff and the visibility of House security personnel. Each of these factors points to an inappropriate employer-employee relationship.

Yet Congress did little to stop unvetted people like Imran and his well-paid band of House contractors from doing all the things Cornell mentioned someone might do.

So little changed that, in 2017, Jim Bacon, a lawyer representing Abid Awan, told the *Washington Post* there was "a very lax environment" in the House of Representatives at the time. "I can tell you what they were doing was not unusual."[10]

That's an understatement. Many IT sources in Congress say Imran and his associates still should have been cleared with background checks by Capitol Police. Even if Imran had originally been investigated when he first began working for congressmen, later background checks should have made Capitol Police open an investigation years sooner. Imran had driving offenses and domestic violence complaints against him, and court records show his mother-in-law accused him of threatening her, of illegally attempting to get life insurance money when his father passed away in Virginia, and of bugging her home. Imran was even involved in a bankruptcy in 2012 (about eight years after he started working for congressmen) while he was being paid about $160,000 a year by Congress.

Financial troubles are a big red flag in background checks for government security clearances. Some of the other key things investigators look into when they are doing a security clearance are connections to foreign countries, associations with unsavory characters, and the person's vulnerability to blackmail. The Awans should have failed all those tests, but then perhaps Capitol Police simply never looked at Imran or his team again after Imran started in 2004—if they even did vet him at that time. Capitol Police's communications director,

Eva Malecki, wouldn't answer even basic questions about how such an investigation works.

Making this even weirder is that Capitol Police allowed Imran to bring in friends and family members who didn't have backgrounds in Information Technology to work as IT administrators for congressmen. Or maybe it's even stranger that these congressmen were willing to sign up IT aides who didn't have any experience. Did they even look at their résumés?

"At the end of the day, whether they had formal training or not, they were trained on the job by Imran," one of Imran Awan's lawyers, Aaron Marr Page, told the *Washington Post*.[11]

But here's the problem: under House rules, independent contractors—which these IT workers were—are prohibited from sharing work, so Imran should have been barred from giving his relations and friends on-the-job training. One reason this is against House rules is because bringing in another person, someone not hired and possibly not even known to the member of Congress and his or her staff, could mean that an unknown IT professional, someone who is not even a government employee, could show up and do things on a computer system that houses a congressman's emails, official calendar, and other personal data. This is like allowing a stranger to walk into your home, a person who simply says he or she knows someone you trust, and then looking the other way as this person goes through your mail and other personal belongings.

"Calendars can pertain to things that are classified," said Rep. Louie Gohmert. "Some foreign countries would pay for congressmen's calendars to see who they are meeting with and what they are saying."

Representative Gohmert said this is especially troubling for elected officials because "we can't do oversight unless we can keep information privilege."[12]

By 2016, these five IT administrators worked for more than three-dozen lawmakers under separate part-time contracts. And they were paid well even if they personally didn't show up for work. The Awan family members each made between $157,000 and $168,000 in 2016, making them among the highest-paid staffers on the Hill.

Imran was being paid "an estimated salary of $165,130" as of 2017, according to Insidegov.com, a salary that was "2.4 times greater than the median for a House staff."[13]

When House Inspector General Cornell was asked about compensation for IT contractors at that 2008 hearing, he said, "[W]e found that the average salary of a financial shared employee, for instance, is one hundred thirty-two thousand dollars. The comparable salary for a CAO [Chief Administrative Office] employee with the same requisite skills and experience would be about sixty-eight thousand dollars."

Compensation for shared IT contractors in congressional offices can vary, as each office is treated as if it's a separate business. But with those glaring differences, it's surprising that more employees don't try to become independent contractors instead—the health plan and 401(k) can't be enough of an incentive to work at less than half pay.

When Rep. Ken Buck (R-CO) was asked for this book how much his office pays for IT support, his staff member Kyle Huwa wrote, "We pay $1,475 for IT Services and $1,860 for CMS Services (IQ House Cloud) for a total of $3,335 per month to Lockheed/Leidos." Lockheed is one of the six preapproved IT firms congressmen are given to choose from; though they don't have to hire someone from the list, most do. The rates Representative Buck's office quoted are typical.

An IT aide who asked to remain anonymous said, "Most House members pay between eleven hundred dollars and fourteen hundred dollars per month. A typical House IT aide patches together work in five to seven offices to make a living this way. Now a member can pay whatever they want, as long as they stay on budget, but it's strange that the Awans were getting more than twice what the typical IT aide gets. I was shocked when I found out how much they were making— that's chief of staff–level pay."

So a single contractor, like Imran, or an IT firm can make more money by picking up more contracts in the House. This means there is a market that private individuals and firms compete for. It is, however, strange that Imran and his crew were somehow so valuable to Democrats in the House that they were willing to pay them much more than the market was offering and that they have not, as this was being written, been compelled to explain why by a House ethics investigation or the mainstream media. This has led some to speculate about just what Imran and his team might also have been doing for these congressmen and/or their staffs.

Still, the fact that shared IT contractors can make more than twice as much as full-time employees who work for Congress, and all are paid with taxpayer money, is just another red flag about this scandal. It is likely some of Imran's team weren't even showing up to work but were instead getting paid six-figure salaries while only a few members of the team did the work.

"What would be the rationale for a member of Congress to pay a twenty-year-old to do nothing? Were there other twenty-year-olds in the House also paid that kind of money?" asked Rep. Ron DeSantis (R-FL) at an informal congressional hearing in October 2017 as he referred to Imran's youngest brother, Jamal.[14]

Maybe, but only a handful of lawmakers have asked questions like that. Even most Republicans have opted not to talk about this deep and complex scandal—many declined interview requests for this book. The few Democrats who have spoken about this case have downplayed the criminal allegations and behaved as if there was no cyber breach. Some have even attacked the few journalists who have written about this scandal in a kill-the-messenger defense. Actually, many are so reluctant to talk about the Awans that a few of the Democrats who'd employed Imran or his team literally ran away when approached in the halls of Congress with questions about their fired IT people.

Just after Imran was arrested in July 2017, Republican National Committee chairwoman Ronna McDaniel did go on *Fox Business* to demand that Democrats explain what this was all about.[15]

McDaniel said, "We have to get to the bottom of this, and Debbie Wasserman Schultz has obstructed at every level on something that affects potentially our national security. So to have this gentleman try and leave the country yesterday, and now we know there is bank fraud and we know he destroyed these hard drives, when you read the story about the Marine that found them in the apartment he was trying to rent. I mean, it is a long story but something we have to get to the bottom of. We are not hearing the Democrats talk about it at all.

Where's Debbie Wasserman Schultz? And we also need to know why the DNC never turned over their hard drive to the FBI to review it as to their hacking situation. So the Democrats are on TV and they're grandstanding every chance they get, but they're not complying and they're not being forthright with their role."

But even McDaniel would soon stop talking about this case—she also declined interview requests for this book.

This silence has resulted in much less pressure than there should be on investigators and those who employed these people, though this hasn't stopped the facts from dribbling out—Capitol Hill is a hard place to keep secrets.

Searches of public databases show there were actually two other "IT professionals" besides the five working on Imran's team. Abid Awan's wife, Natalia Soba, a Russian-speaking woman from Ukraine, also worked for a while as an IT person for congressional offices. She is actually the only member of the group who is not from Pakistan.

Haseeb Rana, a friend of Imran, also worked with the group. Luke Rosiak of the *Daily Caller* referred to Rana as a "patsy"[16] tasked with doing a lot of the IT work the high-paid Awan brothers were supposed to be doing. Rana earned an estimated salary of $85,028 as a shared employee in 2015, or $16,728 more than the median for a House staffer, according to InsideGov.com.[17] Rana was employed in Congress between 2013 and 2015. He was listed as a staffer for Rep. David Loebsack (D-IA), Rep. Emanuel Cleaver (D-MO), Rep. Joe Garcia (D-FL), Rep. Julia Brownley (D-CA), Rep. Kyrsten Sinema (D-AZ), and Rep. Robin Kelly (D-IL).

Sources say Rana quit because he was tired of doing much of the work for about half the salary his colleagues were making.

Meanwhile, Imran's friend Rao Abbas (the man who had previously worked as a manager at a McDonald's and who started working for congressmen as an IT professional in 2012) lived in the basement of a house that Hina Alvi, Imran's wife, owned as a rental property. Cristal Perpignan, a tenant who lived on the top floors of this same house, related this part of the story.

Abbas made a salary of $93,151 as a House IT administrator in 2016. When he was booted off the congressional system with the others on February 2, 2017, he was working as shared staffer for Rep. Emanuel Cleaver (D-MO), Rep. John Sarbanes (D-MD), Rep. Joseph Crowley (D-NY), and Rep. Patrick Murphy (D-PA).

"Rao [Abbas] appeared to be home on most days," said Perpignan. She claimed that Imran told her Abbas had lost his job at McDonald's. Imran, she says, even told her to make the rental checks payable to Abbas instead of Imran's wife, Hina Alvi, who would have officially been the landlord at the time. The financial arrangements in this family were always complicated, with many of them living in the same homes in the Washington metro area as the checks flowed in from Congress.

If Abbas didn't actually perform IT work for these congressmen— interestingly, for several years Abbas is listed on official pay records as the *only* IT worker for Rep. Emanuel Cleaver—it should make investigators wonder whether someone else, such as maybe Imran, did the IT work for the congressman as Abbas got paid a six-figure salary. (If Congress ever does hold an investigative hearing on this, Representative Cleaver should be called and asked just who was doing his office's IT work.)

Still, a congressional IT aide who asked to remain anonymous said, "IT administrators often stay in the background. They are asked to come in and quietly get a computer working or something, and then they go. But then, what I can't answer is who these offices were calling and why a chief of staff wouldn't think it strange that, when they did call for IT support, someone they weren't paying would show to do the work, which is against House rules. They should have realized there were ghost employees being paid exorbitant salaries with public funds."

There is a paper trail. To get administrator-level access to a congressional office's accounts, according to House rules, a form has to be submitted that requires the member's signature. If these forms weren't filled out, Capitol Police could go after a congressman's chief of staff for the infraction and use it as leverage to get them talking about just who was showing up to do the IT work. If these forms were filled out, they would quickly know who was supposed to be there and could match up the work with other known factors, such as their travel histories. Yet, as this was being written, this part of the investigation had dragged on for over a year without charges being filed.

What makes this part of the case so clear is the fact that people who are not on staff are not allowed to do work in a congressional office, which makes sense, as a congressman wouldn't need to be hacked if anyone could just show up and simply say "hi" as they log in to that member's computer system and download everything they want onto a flash drive.

There were a lot of strange arrangements on these congressional staffs. For example, Rep. Ted Deutch (D-FL) had Natalia Soba as his IT person in 2011. Soon he had Natalia, Imran, and Abbas all listed as working for his office, which is an awful lot of IT support for a single congressman. For the last two years before the jig was up, only Abbas was listed as an employee—so again, if Abbas was a no-show employee, it should have been obvious to the staff. Representative Deutch's chief of staff would have had to call someone when their staff needed an email account set up or if a printer malfunctioned. It's not likely that a congressional office would go two years without ever needing an IT administrator to open or close an email account or perform other routine services.

So, with allegedly no-show employees connected to Imran being added as they got on the payrolls of more congressional offices, and with them working in complex webs for many Democrats, someone had to do the actual IT work. This is why Imran likely enlisted his friend Haseeb Rana to do a lot of this work. Rana is the one Rosiak called a "patsy."

Haseeb's father, Tanwir Rana, agrees with this claim. Tanwir said his son is a skilled IT professional and that "they made him do all the work.... After three months, he wanted to leave. We were having a very charged relationship with Imran. [Haseeb] was not satisfied with their behavior."[18]

Haseeb, as noted earlier, was making about half as much as those who were likely shadow employees.

It's also strange that Haseeb's father said Imran had "hired" Haseeb. Legally, all of these people were independent contractors. If Imran had formed a company, and then paid taxes that way, he and his associates would ironically have been subject to a lot more oversight than they were as independent contractors. Congress, as it turns out, had bigger holes in its system than the DNC did in the 2016 election cycle, and Imran exploited them expertly and with cover from congressmen and their staffs.

The fact that Rep. Debbie Wasserman Schultz declined to fire Imran even after he was banned from Congress's computer system for providing fraudulent data to Capitol Police prompted the Foundation for Accountability and Civic Trust (FACT) to petition Congress to open an ethics investigation into Representative Wasserman Schultz and other Democrats who'd employed Imran Awan and his associates.

"I don't understand why Congress isn't already holding hearings looking into this mess," said Kendra Arnold, general counsel for FACT. "Typically, it takes Congress two to three months to let us know whether they will open an ethics inquiry. There is so much going on here that smells, but whatever investigators unearth, it is clear that Representative Wasserman Schultz is in violation of House ethics rules, as members of Congress are directly responsible for ensuring their staffs are only paid for official public work."[19]

As this book was going to print, months had passed but Congress still hadn't answered FACT to say whether an ethics investigation will take place. Also, there had only been one brief informal hearing in Congress attended by a few concerned Republican congressmen to look into this matter. To a large extent, it's been clear that both parties would like this story to go away.

This is especially alarming when you realize that several congressional IT aides told the Daily Caller News Foundation's investigative group that "members of Congress have displayed an inexplicable and intense loyalty towards the suspects who police say victimized them. The baffled aides wonder if the suspects are blackmailing representatives based on the contents of their emails and files, to which they had full access."[20]

An IT aide contacted for this book who has worked for members of Congress for more than a decade said, "I know people who approached the congressional offices Imran and the others worked for and offered services at one-fourth the price of the Awans, but the members said no thanks. At the time, I couldn't understand why these offers were being turned down, but now I think the Awans had some leverage over members."

Other House IT professionals spoken with for this book made similar claims and explained that an IT person could easily have copies of a congressman's emails and other data that they could use to buy silence.

"I'm not sure what they have, but they have something on staffers or members," said one IT aide. "It's crazy. If I was accused of just *some* of what these people are accused of, I'd be taken out in handcuffs."

Reports of Thefts Didn't Even Make Capitol Police Act

Exorbitant salaries for possible no-show employees are just one facet of what was going on in these congressional offices. Actually, Imran must be a quick study, as within a few years of emigrating from Pakistan he'd sized up Washington and found its oversights, its largess, and its biases to be the mad rules of a game he could play. He might have thought that if the Department of Defense could approve a $283,500 grant to monitor the lives of gnatcatchers, and if the US National Institutes of Health can pay some grad student $48,500 to write a history of smoking in Russia, and if the Government Accountability Office says five federal agencies alone spent $3.1 billion on workers placed on administrative leave over just two years,[21] then he could easily get away with committing perhaps hundreds of thousands of dollars in theft and fraud.

But then, like a lot of gamblers, Imran's biggest problem is he didn't know when to stop pushing his luck—the silver lining here is that his greed and actions opened a window for us to see much bigger problems.

We know, for example, some of the details of what happened in one congressional office (out of more than forty). A chief of staff—we don't know which one, as there was a staff change during the period in which this occurred—for Rep. Yvette Clarke (D-NY) agreed to a request from Abid Awan in early 2016 to sign away $120,000 in missing computer equipment. Clarke's chief of staff quietly wrote off the loss of the public equipment worth tens of thousands of dollars in public money and prevented it from coming up in future audits by signing a form removing the missing equipment from a House-wide tracking system.

The missing equipment tied to Clarke's office included a lot of iPhones and iPads, say sources familiar with the matter. At between five hundred and one thousand dollars apiece, the written-off equipment added up fast. Actually, before long it would have been enough to supply over a hundred employees with iPads or iPhones, yet the office only had sixteen employees at the time, according to official payroll records.

Incredibly, the tens of thousands of taxpayers' dollars stolen from Congress is "not the highest of our concerns," Rep. Steve King (R-IA) told *WND* in an interview.[22] "The American people deserve to know the truth to this; it is a big deal. It's not just $6 or $7 million, $120,000 worth of equipment here or there. The biggest thing is that the brothers, Awan's wife, and friend all had access to the private emails and electronic communications of members of Congress and all their staff."

King also said there's "no telling what they downloaded, what they know."

"They've had access to all of the computers of about sixty Democratic House members," he said. "The access of that information would not have been limited. They would have had the passwords for all of those members of Congress."

Nevertheless, Abid Awan would keep his job in the office even after this $120,000 loss became known to Representative Clarke's chief of staff. Actually, the chief of staff didn't tell investigators when it was written off but only talked about it after House administrators later caught wind of the matter around February 2016 and opened an investigation into the Awans.

Wendy Anderson, had taken over for Shelley Davis as Clarke's chief of staff in February 2016, which was the same month Abid Awan allegedly requested the massive write-off for the equipment, so official pay records don't make it clear whether it was Davis or Anderson who signed the form. Sources do say, however, that Anderson knew it occurred, as she had notified House authorities of the $120,000 write-off when they asked whether she'd noticed any problems with expenditures.[23] And it seems safe to presume that Capitol Police are now aware who signed the form.

In an informal congressional hearing on this matter in October 2017, Rep. Louie Gohmert said he once had trouble writing off "an old typewriter" from "the 1980s" that he had never seen and "a couch purchased in 1976" by a previous member that he had never sat on, so he said with incredulity, "I read with interest that a member could write off one hundred twenty thousand dollars."[24]

And this is just one example from one congressman's office. We don't know what happened in the forty or so other offices that employed this crew of IT people. Also, as this was being written over a year after House administrators became aware of the situation, no charges have yet been filed related to all the missing iPads, iPhones, and other equipment.

To be blunt, the Awan brothers are suspected of having run a fraud scheme in which offices would purchase equipment in a way that was designed to avoid in-house tracking. Sources say they're being investigated for possibly working with an employee of CDW•G Inc., one of the Hill's largest technology providers, to alter invoices to avoid oversight by House administrators. They did this by allegedly billing the House for just less than $500, since anything costing $500 or more has to be tracked by House administrators. To get an item off this list—like Representative Gohmert's antique typewriter—someone would have to fill out more paperwork. Sources speculate that the goal of the scheme was to remove and sell the equipment outside of Congress. Some of the equipment, according to sources, never reached Congress; instead, it was mailed to homes owned by the Awans.

Kelly Caraher, the spokesperson for CDW•G Inc., answered media requests to say the company has been cooperating with investigators. She also said, "The prosecutors directing this investigation have informed CDW and its coworkers that they are not subjects or targets of the investigation."

If that is true, why would Capitol Police grant them this assurance? Police don't typically walk around telling people they are innocent. Investigators are supposed to investigate and prosecutors are supposed to then look at what investigators gather as they decide whether to press charges. Also, an assurance of innocence from the authorities could later be used in court to dispute charges even after new evidence turned up.

We do know that official employment records show Abid stayed on Representative Clarke's staff until September 2016, or about six months after the $120,000 loss was acknowledged and written off. Records also show that since she got into office in 2007, Clarke's IT administrator position had been variously filled by Imran, Hina, and Abid. It doesn't seem likely that she fired Imran or Hina Alvi and then hired Imran's unskilled brother to do the work. Obviously, Imran and Hina Alvi had reached the salary cap and brought in Abid to be paid by Clarke as they took over IT in other Democrats' offices. So then, was Abid even showing up, or was Imran or someone else still doing the work? Representative Clarke's office declined media requests to explain.

Another facet to this odd and dangerous arrangement might explain why all this equipment was quietly written off. Members of Congress can actually be found personally liable for money or equipment that goes missing from their taxpayer-funded offices. The write-off process exists through the House chief administrative officer because a congressman shouldn't reasonably be financially liable just because a staffer misplaced an iPhone. So this write-off process was established to balance the books in cases of such small, unintentional discrepancies. A $120,00 write-off, of course, is no small discrepancy but actually would be enough money for a member of Congress to pay several staffers for a year.

Perhaps $120,000 is a small amount compared to what was actually taken, however, because the figure covers only Representative Clarke's office. Imran and his associates worked for more than forty members of Congress. If investigators have looked at the books of these other offices, they haven't yet said what they've found. Once again, this whole investigation has the feel of a cover-up.

We do know that congressional investigators have looked into at least some of the transactions the Awans made. Back in March 2016, auditors working for the House's chief administrative officer discovered the odd invoices for computer equipment. After a referral to the House inspector general's office, the *Washington Post* reported that investigators found the Awans had asked vendors "to split the cost of equipment among multiple items and charged these items as office supplies instead of equipment," according to a September 2016 briefing document. "As of Sept. 1, 2016, there had been 34 purchases totaling nearly $38,000 'where the costs of the item was manipulated to obtain a purchase price of $499.99,' according to the document. There were $799 iPads and a $640 television on the list, records show."[25]

It isn't as if there isn't a paper trail for investigators to follow. A member of Congress or a high-level staffer with financial responsibility would have had to sign off on all of these vouchers, at least if they expected the money to be paid.

This paper trail of accountability also raises questions about how an office staff wouldn't have noticed equipment that was being purchased but never actually showed up for them to use. Anyone who has worked in an office knows there can be jealousy and excitement when a person or division gets new computers or smartphones. Offices are always abuzz with which printer is working and who dominates the copier. It is hard to believe that the typically young, college-educated, and social-media-loving professionals who work in congressional offices wouldn't have noticed who had what gadget. And it is not a believable narrative that a chief of staff, or whoever had the responsibility to sign these vouchers, wouldn't have noticed that the stuff either was disappearing or never showing up in the first place.

Then There Was a Car Dealership

Investigators should have also noticed that there were clear signs the Awans needed money to fuel their failed business ventures, credit card debt, and love of real estate. For example, as he earned about

$160,000 a year from Congress, Abid Awan also ran a car dealership in Virginia that went bankrupt in a loud way in 2012. Abid actually filed for bankruptcy to get rid of massive debts related to this failed business, though he was somehow working full time for Congress at the time.

This car dealership was hardly a secret shell company entwined in the complexities of corporate and international law. Investigators should have had no problem seeing that Abid and Imran were in major financial trouble as they managed IT for congressmen—bankruptcies and other large debts are some of the first things investigators look into when they do background checks for security purposes. Even a Realtor or any authorized person with web access can check credit scores, and these people's scores must have fallen into a hole with the bankruptcy. One would think that those in charge of administrative oversight would have kept tabs on IT administrator positions that gave people access to all of a congressman's emails (both sent and received) and to other personal and official data. There are, after all, publicly viewable court records that detail Abid's bankruptcy and that even connect him to an Iranian who fled justice in the United States by fleeing to Iraq.

Abid's car dealership was called Cars International A in court records (ironically, in this very international plot, it abbreviated as "CIA"), though some refer to it just as "Cars International." It was located in Falls Church, Virginia, and was in business from November 2009 to September 2010, according to the bankruptcy filing. Abid declared $1,141,850 in debt when he filed for bankruptcy in 2012.[26] Weirdly, Abid said in the filing that a car of his, worth $38,199, had been repossessed in 2009 (the same year he started the dealership), so he lost a car to creditors and then found a way to get a whole lot full of them. He also listed tens of thousands of dollars in credit card debt and "possible" unknown costs related to lawsuits that might be filed by people who were financially harmed by Cars International A's quick implosion.

This was a contentious bankruptcy. Abid's business associates accused him in court documents of stealing money and vehicles from them and said the dealership's financial books were incomprehensible. Another car dealer who supplied Abid's business with cars said that Abid had not paid for the vehicles and wouldn't return them. "The consignment agreements state it clearly that either Mr. Awan sells the cars for the agreed price [of] no less $62,200 or return my cars back," he wrote.

These kinds of financial disagreements occur all the time in small-claims courts across the nation, where someone just really doesn't think they should have to pay for their decisions. The differences here are the huge sums of money squandered in so short a time—over $1 million in about two years—and the fact that, even though Abid filed for bankruptcy in 2012 to deal with his intertwined mix of personal and business debts, he somehow managed to keep ownership of two homes while telling the bankruptcy court, as well as the people he owed tens of thousands of dollars to, that he had no assets to pay them with. In the filing, he claimed that his home in Annandale, Virginia, which was valued at $408,000, and one with tenants that he said was worth $380,000, shouldn't be liquidated because he and his wife, Natalia Soba, were living apart and needed separate residences.

"My spouse and I are legally separated under applicable non-bankruptcy law or my spouse and I are living apart other than for the purpose of evading the requirements of § 707(b)(2)(A) of the Bankruptcy Code," Abid declared in the bankruptcy documents.

Maybe the court thought that subsequent civil actions would sort this out, as Abid even lists in the filing that "unknown" costs are sure to come from unhappy creditors, but for some reason they let Abid get away with keeping his homes. They did this even though the bankruptcy meant that several small businesses and individuals likely wouldn't get paid back.

One of these individuals is especially interesting. A court deposition says the car dealership took $100,000 from Ali al-Attar, an Iranian physician who was raised in Iraq and who, as this was going to print, was wanted by the US Department of Justice.

In March 2012, a federal grand jury indicted a cardiologist, Abdul H. Fadul, along with al-Attar, a doctor of internal medicine who had worked in Alexandria and McLean, Virginia.[27] The jury indicted them on charges of conspiracy to defraud the United States by attempting to hide their true income and for preparing false tax returns.

Fadul and al-Attar, according to the indictment, held joint ownership interests in nine medical practices located in Maryland and Virginia. Each practice had its own bank account. For tax years 2004 and 2005, Fadul and al-Attar engaged an accounting firm in Maryland to prepare income tax returns for themselves and the joint medical practices. The defendants advised the accounting firm that it was standard procedure for each of the medical practices to deposit the business receipts it generated, including payments from patients and insurance companies, into its own bank account. Then, on March 26, 2004, Fadul and al-Attar opened a joint bank account in their own names, into which they began depositing business receipts without telling their accountants.

The five-count indictment alleges that from March 26, 2004, through July 12, 2006, Fadul and al-Attar conspired to defraud the United States by concealing their total income. Specifically, Fadul and al-Attar deposited over $500,000 in checks from patients and insurance companies for medical services rendered into the joint account in their names rather than into the bank accounts of the medical practices that had generated the payments. The defendants then allegedly spent the money on personal items, including real estate and other personal investments. Possibly one of these investments was to fund the Awans' car dealership.

Al-Attar quickly fled the United States for Iraq to avoid what prosecutors said could result in him being locked up for three years in a federal penitentiary. Al-Attar has a long history with Iraq. He was born in Iraq to Iranian parents and was a 1989 graduate of the American University of Beirut Faculty of Medicine.[28] He soon immigrated to the United States and set up a practice in internal medicine in Greenbelt, Maryland, a suburb of Washington. Al-Attar eventually expanded his business to include nine practices that he wholly or partly owned in Virginia and Maryland.

Philip Giraldi, a former CIA officer and currently executive director of the Council for the National Interest, wrote that "al-Attar was investigated by the FBI and eventually indicted for large scale health care fraud in 2008–09. This included charging insurance companies more than $2.3 million for services their patients did not actually receive, with many of the false claims using names of diplomats and employees enrolled in a group plan at the Egyptian Embassy in Washington. In one case, the doctors claimed an embassy employee visited three of their clinics every twenty-six days between May 2007 and August 2008 to have the same testing done each time. The insurance company paid the doctors $55,000 for more than four hundred nonexistent procedures for the one patient alone."[29]

The FBI raided al-Attar's offices in 2009, and the Department of Health and Human Services sued his business partner in 2011.[30] After al-Attar fled justice in the United States, he was spotted late in 2012 "in Beirut, Lebanon, conversing with a Hezbollah official."[31]

But al-Attar was more than just a shady doctor. Before his indictment, al-Attar had a dubious relationship with the George W. Bush administration before the 2003 US invasion of Iraq. He promoted himself as a leader of Iraqi dissidents opposed to Saddam Hussein, and he did seem to have had a lot of influence in those circles. Giraldi, the former CIA officer, wrote in the *American Conservative* in 2013 that al-Attar informed President Bush's Iraq policy advisors that US forces would be "greeted as liberators."[32] Also, in "late 2002 and early 2003, [then-Deputy Secretary of Defense Paul] Wolfowitz regularly met secretly with a group of Iraqi expatriates, consisting mostly of Shias but also including several Sunnis, who resided in the Washington area," said Giraldi. "The Iraqis were headed by one Dr. Ali A. al-Attar."

Al-Attar's prediction was disastrously wrong, and his qualifications for making it—allegedly based on what he and other Iraqis in the United States were hearing from relatives in Iraq—seem dubious, as al-Attar's parents were Iranian. Nevertheless, the US-backed regime change in Iraq benefited al-Attar, at least in the short term, as in 2003 he told *The New York Times* he was one of four people chosen by General Garner to re-establish the Iraq Ministry of Health, and that he expected to be called to Baghdad the following week.[33]

Such were some of the business associates of Imran Awan and his family members. As you'll see later, Imran also paid police officers in

Pakistan for things that are still unclear and had other associations that should have worried Capitol Police.

During Abid's bankruptcy, Nasir Khattak, who ran a car dealership called AAA and who acted as an intermediary between al-Attar and the Awans, said in a deposition related to the bankruptcy filing: "It was very bad record-keeping in Cars International...it is close to impossible to make any sense out of all the transactions that happened."[34]

Khattak also said Cars International A was a "family business" and that by 2010 Imran was its primary manager instead of Abid. Because their finances were intertwined, Imran was also a big part of this bankruptcy.

Reading Nasir Khattak's deposition, filed in the Circuit Court of Fairfax County, Virginia, is like trying to make sense of Bernie Madoff's juggled finances. There are competing financial statements; cars moved informally between Khattak's car dealership and the Awans; various loans made from al-Attar, via Khattak, to the Awans; and even a possible change of ownership due to the failure of the Awans to repay the loans. There are other partners and so many nonsensical statements, the person deposing Khattak is clearly exasperated on several occasions as he tries to get straight answers. Though Khattak oversaw the loans from al-Attar and should have been able to factually explain how much money was owed to al-Attar, he often doesn't have clear answers, and when he is repeatedly asked to give specifics, he cannot. The finances are so interwoven and unclear that no one can sort out how this dealership, Cars International A, was ever to make sense, much less a profit. This is perhaps the biggest reason Abid was able to keep his homes.

All of this went down publicly in court, yet Capitol Police were either oblivious or didn't think it mattered that a group of Pakistan-born immigrants who desperately needed money, some of whom reports say often traveled back to Pakistan for long stays, had access to reams of data from forty or more United States congressmen?

Toward the end, Capitol Police eventually *were* watching as these IT administrators did strange and quite possibly illegal things on the House network, yet they still didn't move in.

If investigators looked, they should have noticed that Abid had several driving- and alcohol-related legal entanglements, including driving with a suspended or revoked license, according to court records. According to the *Daily Caller*, Abid was actually "found guilty of drunk driving a month before he started at the House and he was arrested for public intoxication a month after his first day,"[35] yet a background check, if one occurred, didn't prevent him from getting on and staying on Congress's payroll.

Imran had also been convicted of driving offenses, such as driving an unregistered vehicle. Nevertheless, the House let these people stay employed as very high-paid IT workers who could see the emails of all of the congressmen they worked for. As this was going to print, Congress has shown almost no interest in investigating.

All of that should have been enough to oust this team of foreign-born IT administrators and possibly put them in jail for theft and fraud, but this next part of the plot should have frightened investigators more than all the other issues combined.

They Were Downloading Terabytes of Data

As the Awans were allegedly stealing equipment from Congress, Capitol Police were watching as the Awans downloaded terabytes of data (a terabyte is 1,024 gigabytes) from congressional offices to a server Capitol Police didn't have access to. The emails, schedules, and more for as many as forty-four congressmen, all Democrats, that Imran Awan and his associates worked for were being copied off-site.

Though this data didn't include records from a separate, classified system, anyone who paid attention during the last election cycle knows how embarrassing or even destructive private emails can be to a politician—or to just about anyone.

Just imagine the panic in the Clinton campaign when WikiLeaks started releasing their emails.

In December 2015, for example, John Podesta, Hillary Clinton's campaign chairman, called Sen. Bernie Sanders (I-VT), who was then Hillary's rival for the DNC's nomination for president, a "doofus."[36]

This would be leaked, and Hillary would later need Sanders's help to win over his supporters. Some Democrats have since complained that Sanders didn't do enough to help Hillary; perhaps this doofus comment was part of the reason.

In September 2015, as Clinton's campaign fretted whether then-vice president Joe Biden would join the Democratic primary race, Podesta wrote: "We've taken on a lot of water that won't be easy to pump out of the boat. Most of that has to do with terrible decisions made pre-campaign, but a lot has to do with her instincts."

Neera Tanden, an adviser, responded, "Almost no one knows better [than] me that her instincts can be terrible."

In the email exchange, Podesta also complained that Hillary's personal lawyer, David Kendall, and former State Department staffers Cheryl Mills and Philippe Reines "sure weren't forthcoming here on the facts here."

To which Tanden said, "Why didn't they get this stuff out like eighteen months ago? So crazy."

Tanden later answered her own question by saying, "I guess I know the answer. They wanted to get away with it."

This might be normal griping for any mid-management team in the throes of a problem, but when such dialogue goes public it can be unseemly. In politics it can also expose lies that destroy campaigns.

When president Barack Obama, for example, told an interviewer he first learned of Hillary's private server at the "same time everybody else learned it, through news reports," the Clinton campaign emailed one another to say that the president wasn't telling the truth. The evening after the interview aired, Clinton spokesman Josh Schwerin said via email that "it looks like POTUS just said he found out HRC was using her personal email when he saw it in the news."[37]

"We need to clean this up," responded Hillary's former chief of staff Cheryl Mills.

"He has emails from her—they do not say state.gov," she wrote.

That emails hacked or leaked can imperil a political career is certainly something Imran's most reliable boss, Rep. Debbie Wasserman Schultz, would have known. It was, after all, emails that were either leaked or hacked that ousted her from her position as the head of the DNC in July 2016.

Representative Wasserman Schultz was elected chairperson of the DNC in 2011, replacing Virginia senator Tim Kaine. On July 24, 2016, Wasserman Schultz announced her resignation from her position after WikiLeaks released 19,252 emails and 8,034 attachments from the DNC, including emails from seven key DNC staff members, dated from January 2015 to May 2016. These emails indicated that they'd worked to sabotage the presidential campaign of Sen. Bernie Sanders in favor of Hillary Clinton's campaign.

Wasserman Schultz's resignation was finalized on July 28 following the 2016 Democratic National Convention. The Florida congresswoman was subsequently appointed honorary chair of the Clinton campaign's "50 state program."

We don't know if the DNC's emails were hacked or leaked because, for some reason, the DNC declined to let the FBI look at its servers. They refused to cooperate with the FBI's computer-forensic experts even as fear that the Russians interfered in the 2016 election, by allegedly helping Trump, dominated the news as Democrats pushed the story. Former FBI director James Comey, among others, confirmed the DNC's stonewalling publicly before he lost his position.[38]

Actually, at the time the DNC told BuzzFeed that the FBI never requested access to its servers after its system was breached.[39] This must have rankled some in the FBI, because the next day a "senior law enforcement official" would say, "The FBI repeatedly stressed to DNC officials the necessity of obtaining direct access to servers and data, only to be rebuffed until well after the initial compromise had been mitigated."[40]

Instead of working with the FBI, the DNC hired CrowdStrike, a private security firm, to look into the breach. This left the FBI with no choice but to rely on a third party, one paid by the DNC, for information about this alleged hack. CrowdStrike would later claim groups that infiltrated the DNC were associated with Russian intelligence, but again, CrowdStrike was paid by the DNC. US intelligence agencies would later repeat this claim by citing CrowdStrike's report, and many on CNN and other media outlets then continually repeated that all the intelligence agencies had said the Russians were behind the release of emails from DNC officials.

That circular reasoning might be what prompted Julian Assange—whose website WikiLeaks published emails from Podesta, Hillary Clinton's campaign chairman—to say on Fox News on January 3, 2017: "We published several Podesta emails, which show Podesta responding to a phishing email. Now how did they respond? Podesta gave out that his password was the word 'password.'... So this is something a fourteen-year-old kid could have hacked."[41]

Now, the data that Imran was copying and moving off-site from the forty or more House Democrats was connected to a server used by the House Democratic Caucus, an organization chaired by then-Rep. Xavier Becerra (D-CA)—another congressman for whom Imran worked.

"The House Office of Inspector General tracked the Awans' network usage and found that a massive amount of data was flowing from the [congressional] networks. Over fifty-seven hundred log-ins by the five Awan associates were discovered on a single server within the House, the server of the Democratic Caucus chairman, then-Representative Xavier Becerra of California," said Rep. Scott Perry (R-PA). "Up to forty or more members of Congress had all of their data moved out of their office servers and onto the Becerra server without their knowledge or consent."[42]

Capitol Police had to take action because Representative Becerra was leaving Congress in January 2017 to become the attorney general of California, and they wanted a copy of that server's contents. Before he left office, Capitol Police informed Becerra that the caucus server was the subject of an investigation and they needed a copy of it.

Becerra presumably told Imran that Capitol Police wanted a copy of the Democratic House Caucus server, though it isn't clear if Becerra said the server's contents were part of an active investigation.

What is known is that Imran did produce a copy of a server for Capitol Police; however, after taking a look at the data they were provided, investigators determined they had been given a copy of some other server. It was a fake. "Capitol Police found that the image [the copy of the server] they were supplied was false," said Representative Perry, quoting a report from the House Office of Inspector General.

"They were using the House Democratic Caucus as their central service warehouse.... It was a breach. The data was completely out of [the members'] possession. Does it mean it was sold to the Russians? I don't know,"[43] a senior official told the *Daily Caller*.

Imran evidently didn't want to turn over this massive amount of evidence, so he supplied a copy of what was supposed to be everything on the server.

"The Awans were either so arrogant they didn't think they'd get caught, or they aren't very skilled," said a cybersecurity expert who asked to have his name kept out of print. "Creating a fake server image to fool investigators just takes a little know-how. What they should have done is create a new copy and then carefully shred the data they didn't want investigators to see. Shredding simply means overwriting the data so many times that it becomes unreadable. Instead of taking the time to do that right, it sounds like they were sloppy. Maybe they even tried to give investigators a copy of a blank server."

Xavier Becerra had paid Imran to manage his personal office server since 2004. He added Hina Alvi, Imran's wife, as a second IT aide in 2013. When Becerra became chairman of the Democratic Caucus in 2013, that office began paying Hina Alvi $25,000 to $30,000 a year in addition to payments from Becerra's personal office. Becerra, in fact, would pay the Awans more than any other congressman.

Later, Hina Alvi would actually be the only IT aide on the payroll of the House Democratic Caucus, a separate setup with its own staff and equipment. Imran and other aides, according to House rules, had no authorization to access the caucus server, but they nevertheless did access it thousands of times, according to a House Office of Inspector General report referenced by Representative Perry.

The log-ins continued for months, and eventually, some close to the investigation say, the entire server disappeared and was replaced with a different server—meaning all the data (evidence) on it vanished.[44] In a plea-deal agreement with Imran Awan, the Department of Justice would later say they then had the "missing" server, but it remained unclear where they got it or if Imran might still have data from it. The Department of Justice would not answer any further questions about this server or about other elements of the case.

During a question-and-answer session at a National Press Club appearance in Washington in December 2017, Becerra refused to answer any questions about the server or the case. Becerra said, "Go back and research your facts, you've got them wrong. I understand that this matter is still under investigation, and we have cooperated with the authorities both within Congress and with the federal government on this."[45]

Becerra's convenient political reaction is in stark contrast to the Democrats' very public rationale for why they lost the 2016 presidential election. They often cite hacks of the DNC's servers that led to WikiLeaks releasing DNC staffers' emails as a central reason for their loss. Now, they have a major cyber breach of their data by an IT aide who worked for Rep. Debbie Wasserman Schultz as she ran the DNC and they don't want to talk about it?

Also, although Democrats, and many left-leaning news outlets, have been quick to say US intelligence agencies agree that Russians were behind the release of DNC officials' emails, and in the process commend the FBI and other US intelligence agencies for their work, the DNC refused to allow the FBI to check out the DNC's servers after the cyber breach became known. In fact, the DNC delayed a response to the FBI after the FBI called to tell them something was afoot.

Donna Brazile, who took over as chairwoman of the DNC from Representative Wasserman Schultz, said that when Wasserman Schultz did communicate news of the breach to DNC leadership weeks after she'd found out about it, her tone was "casual." According to Brazile, Wasserman Schultz waited until just before she knew the *Washington Post* was going with a story on the breach in June 2016 before she finally held a conference call to tell DNC leadership about the crisis—a cyber breach they would later say cost them the election.

Brazile wrote in her book, *Hacks: The Inside Story of Break-Ins and Breakdowns That Put Donald Trump in the White House*:

On June 14 Debbie invited the Democratic Party officers to a conference call to alert us that a story about hacking the DNC would be published in the *Washington Post* the following day. That call was the first time we'd heard that there was a problem. Debbie's tone was so casual that I had not absorbed the details, nor even thought that it was much for us to be concerned about. Her manner indicated that this hacking thing was something she had covered. But had she?

Brazile also said that two top Obama administration officials told her the DNC had rebuffed the FBI's offers to help deal with the hack. Brazile wrote that Susan Rice "told me I had to take this very seriously." Nevertheless, Brazile says that Rice told her, "It took a long time for the FBI to get any response from the party. Make sure that the DNC cooperates fully with the investigators, promise me that." Brazile even says that Eric Holder, then the attorney general, told her "the DNC was not very responsive to the FBI."

When asked to apologize to donors and others who'd been harmed by the breach, Brazile says Representative Wasserman Schultz said, "I'm not doing that."[46]

Whether the DNC leak had anything to do with Imran Awan and what he and others were up to on the House Democratic Caucus server is speculation without clear evidence as this was being written, but it is clear why Becerra likely doesn't want to talk about this investigation. Becerra had first hired Imran in 2004, and congressional pay records show he was one of the Awans' best employers. So looking into Imran's activities in 2016, and before, would raise questions about more than a decade of the Democrats' data. It would also raise questions as to why Becerra didn't see or act on the warning signs about the Awans. Becerra and his staff should have clearly seen that Imran was a textbook example of an insider threat; if they did, for reasons we don't yet know, they didn't take basic security measures to protect their data.

Part of the reason people such as Becerra don't feel compelled to speak is that the media have been giving them cover. After what the Awans were up to on the House Democratic Caucus server became public knowledge, the *Washington Post* tried to downplay the massive data breach by reporting that "according to a senior congressional official familiar with the probe, criminal investigators have found no evidence that the IT workers had any connection to a foreign government. Investigators looking for clues about espionage instead found that the workers were using one congressional server as if it were their home computer, storing personal information such as children's homework and family photos, the official said."[47]

This *Washington Post* reporter just danced past this crazy claim as if to say, sure, children's homework and family photos can easily amount to terabytes of data.

This is such an absurd oversight that it's hard to quantify, as terabytes can be hard to visualize. To give it some perspective, realize that the complete works of William Shakespeare would take up about five megabytes of space in plain text format, whereas a terabyte) is a million times bigger than a megabyte. It was a big deal in 2007 when Hitachi introduced the world's first one-terabyte hard-disk drive. To give this a physical dimension, realize that to store one terabyte of data it would take about 1,428 CD-ROMs, 212 DVDs, or 40 single-player Blu-ray Discs. Put another way, to fill a terabyte with family photos, a person would need about a quarter of a million photos.

Yet the *Washington Post* didn't challenge the claim that this data was just homework and family photos?

It was no big deal to the *Post* that, according to Rep. Scott Perry, Imran and possibly some others on his team logged in to the server more than 5,700 times. About 5,400 of those log-ins appear to be unauthorized, says a report by the House inspector general, as only Hina Alvi was authorized to log in to that server, yet 5,400 of the log-ins were made by Imran and the others. That server, Representative Perry said, actually belonged to Representative Becerra.

Also, why would a congressional staffer upload his children's homework and family photos to a congressman's server? Cloud services, such as Google Photos, provide that kind of service. The congressional server in question had no monitor, so it wasn't like an IT aide could view the photos on it. So then, why would the Awans upload personal data from a home computer onto a House server when they would have to download it again when they wanted to see the images or other documents?

Hina Alvi, who was authorized to upload things to the server, could have uploaded pictures of her children without attracting attention, but again, why would she?

The *Post* reported:

> By midsummer [2016], with the approval of the House Administration Committee, the Inspector General's Office was tracking the five employees' logins. In October, they found "massive" amounts of data flowing from the networks they were accessing, raising the possibility that an automated program was vacuuming up information, according to a senior House official familiar with the probe. Initially, investigators could not see precisely what kind of data was moving off the server due to legal protections afforded by the Constitution's "speech and debate" clause, which shields lawmakers' deliberations from investigators' eyes. Investigators found that the five IT employees had logged on at one server for the Democratic Caucus more than 5,700 times over a seven-month period, according to documents reviewed by *The Post*. Alvi, the only one of the five who was authorized to access that server, accounted for fewer than 300 of those logins, documents show.

This mention of the "speech and debate" clause suggests that Democrats barred Capitol Police from looking at the apparent data breach. The *Post* has printed a lot of cover stories about cybersecurity and hacks they argue were done by Russians, yet they say questions about what happened on this server are "unfounded conspiracy theories and intrigue"?

Despite how the *Post* downplayed this case, what Imran and/or his associates were doing was very unusual, likely illegal, and contrary to congressional procedures. According to sources in Congress, each House member's data is supposed to be stored on his or her own server, but Imran moved all of their files to a computer that was supposed to only hold files for the administrative office of the House Democratic Caucus.

Nevertheless, many of the Democrats who'd hired Imran and his team have either refused to comment on the case or have said their data wasn't compromised. According to the House inspector general, it was clearly copied and moved off-site or out of their control. Isn't that the definition of being compromised?

The hypocrisy runs so deep here that, though some of the members of Congress who employed Imran or one of his associates have argued the Awans weren't authorized to see classified materials, eight Democrats on the House Intelligence Committee actually asked for their staffers to have this access to classified materials. On March 22, 2016, the Democrats wrote a letter to an appropriations subcommittee seeking $125,000 in additional funding so their staffers could obtain "Top Secret—Sensitive Compartmented Information" clearances. This is the highest-level security classification. Imran, or one of his associates, was working for several of the Democrats who signed this letter. The letter was sent to Rep. Debbie Wasserman Schultz, ranking member of the House Appropriations Committee's Subcommittee on the Legislative Branch, and to Rep. Tom Graves (R-GA), the subcommittee's chairman.[48]

Would these eight members make such a request without communicating with higher-ranking members in their party? This is important, as the Awans weren't just backing up these congressmen's data on the server. Soon it would come out that data was also backed up to Dropbox on a massive scale. Congressional offices are actually prohibited from using Dropbox because it's an off-site consumer product. Awan might have had access to any data stored on Dropbox even after he was banned from the congressional network. He could have copied it and still could hold it on a flash drive or other device.

Perhaps the members of Congress who had employed Imran and his associates aren't talking due to fear over something they might have said via their emails, or something that was or might be in their in-boxes. Many Democrats even began refusing to acknowledge the cybersecurity breach had taken place. Representative Wasserman Schultz and others have also declined to even criticize the suspects, though this team of IT people from Pakistan has been accused of a lot more than the bank fraud Imran and Hina Alvi would be indicted for in August 2017.

As this was going on, Becerra left for California with his chief of staff and former executive director of the Democratic Caucus, Sean McCluskie. McCluskie earned an estimated salary of $172,500 working for Becerra,[49] or just a little more than Imran and his associates were making while they were employed by members of Congress. McCluskie left with Becerra to be chief deputy attorney general of California. He and Becerra both declined to comment on what Imran did and why he backed up all of the emails and other data from so many congressmen on the caucus server and, according to congressional reports, a Dropbox account.

Finally, Capitol Police Act

On February 2, 2017, House sergeant-at-arms Paul Irving finally banned Imran and his associates from the House network. The image of the fake server provided to Capitol Police by Imran was the final straw. Irving must have realized that if Imran and the others involved were willing to obstruct justice this brazenly, then there was no telling what they might have done or what they might do.

On that day, Irving, House chief administrative officer Phil Kiko, and Jamie Fleet, the Democratic staff director of the Committee on House Administration, asked all the chiefs of staff working for the members of Congress who'd employed Imran and his crew to a meeting.

When they gathered, the chiefs of staff were told that this team of IT aides was banned from the House network. Because these IT administrators only worked for Democrats, no Republican staffer was present. This ensured that, from the beginning, the breach would be hushed up politically; in fact, in the briefing the House officials didn't mention the cybersecurity breach that had occurred or other key details about what this team of IT aides had been up to on the House system.

The next day, February 3, 2017, Committee on House Administration chairman Gregg Harper (R-MS) and ranking member Robert Brady (D-PA) would issue the only official statement about what the statement calls "the ongoing House theft investigation."[50]

"House Officials became aware of suspicious activity and alleged theft committed by certain House IT support staff," the statement read. "An internal investigation determined that a number of House policies and procedures had been violated. This information was turned over to the United States Capitol Police and their investigation is ongoing. These employees have also been blocked from accessing House systems. All offices impacted have been contacted. No further comment will be issued until the investigation is complete."

When the chiefs of staff then informed their congressmen that the Awans and their accomplices had been banned from the House network, many of the members of Congress began firing this team of IT administrators from Pakistan.

"After being notified by the House Administration Committee, this individual was removed from our payroll. We are confident that everything in our office is secure,"[51] said a spokesman for Rep. Sander Levin (D-MI). But then, Levin's chief of staff, Nick Gwyn, didn't explain how the secret server and Dropbox accounts were "secure."

In another example, a spokesman for Rep. Marcia Fudge (D-OH) said she fired Imran after learning of the criminal investigation but claimed "there's no indication that he stole information or did anything inappropriate."[52] She said this even though it is widely acknowledged that Imran copied her office's information and kept it on a server and possibly a Dropbox account she had no control over.

Rep. Scott Perry would later call these "massive" data transfers on government servers by Imran "a substantial security threat."[53] Perry, a member of the Homeland Security subcommittee on cybersecurity, said that the House Office of Inspector General tracked the network usage of Imran and his associates on House servers as terabytes of data were moving off the network.

Still, many of the congressmen who'd employed the Awans wouldn't even acknowledge that a security breach had occurred. As a result, it's hard to say whether they took action to investigate where their data might have gone or to prevent future violations of their personal and official data.

Rep. Debbie Wasserman Schultz did acknowledge that chiefs of staff were informed the Awans were under investigation for what she referred to as "data transfer violations."[54] Nevertheless, she declined to fire Imran even after he was banned from the House network—she would keep giving Imran public money, then as a consultant since he could no longer legally get on Congress's network, until he was arrested about six months later, in July.

This sent many congressmen searching for new IT workers, which led to some other telling interactions. An IT contractor who asked not to have his name printed claimed that, after Imran and his team were banned from the House network, he approached some of these offices but was told they weren't interested in hiring him. He speculates that some of the congressmen or their staffs might believe he was an informant for Capitol Police, though he says he wasn't. This is a little like the honor code among prisoners where, though laws might be broken by those on the inside, snitching is punished. Perhaps this isn't all that surprising, as people who work in the federal bureaucracy are well aware that whistleblowing is career suicide.

Some of the House IT professionals contacted for this book, who all wanted to remain anonymous, said that while the Awans worked for dozens of congressional offices, they never attended regular IT networker meetings that most IT professionals who work for these offices do attend. They also said the Awans never took part in an IT email group that helps these contractors solve problems and stay up with House rules.

"When you're an admin for an office you have access to everything; you're the one providing access for staffers," said an IT specialist.

How did that not cause Capitol Police or the House inspector general to take notice? Here Congress had a group of IT people making huge salaries well over the norm, not taking part in normal administrative meetings, and sharing their responsibilities in ways that break House rules, all as they likely stole perhaps hundreds of thousands of dollars' worth of equipment and copied terabytes of data, yet Capitol Police didn't act for years?

The fact that Imran and his associates could read all the emails dozens of members of Congress sent and received, as well as had access to many of the official files congressmen and their staffs stored, should have made House authorities do something. Meanwhile, Imran's own stepmother said in court documents that they often sent money to Pakistan and that Imran frequently, and for months at a time, traveled to Pakistan, a country with well-substantiated ties to the Taliban and al-Qaeda.[55]

None of these people, who were still under investigation as this was being written, are natural-born citizens of the United States. Imran is a naturalized citizen. It's unclear if the others are naturalized citizens or merely green card holders. This fact by itself should have made Capitol Police take notice at a time when the media was going hyperbolic about foreign governments trying to influence a US presidential election. Now sure, profiling people based on their ethnicity or religion is a politically correct no-no, but common sense shouldn't be off-limits for police officers.

Oddly, though, none of the people tracked down and interviewed for this book said the FBI had spoken to them. There doesn't seem to be much of an investigation going on, and there is even less being reported in the media.

Journalist Luke Rosiak wondered in an informal congressional hearing on this case if there is a "kickback scheme" somewhere causing congressmen and/or their staffers to basically plead the Fifth. Was Imran's team sharing proceeds from missing computer equipment or their large salaries with congressmen or their staffs?

A conspiracy that large among dozens of congressional offices seems far-fetched. There are 435 members of the House who employee about 8,000 staff members.[56] As the average congressman has a full-time staff of about 14 people, this would mean that over 600 people (actually many more, as staffers come and go) interacted with Imran and his associates while they were at their height. Staffers are used to speaking with the media and among each other. Leaks are normal from these mostly young and well-educated people. Staffs of different members meet in lunchrooms, at many Capitol Hill functions and parties, and elsewhere, where they mingle with journalists and lobbyists. It is hard to imagine a secret kickback scheme involving even a fraction of these people remaining a secret for long.

From a journalist's perspective, this weakness in our big and cumbersome system—with two houses of Congress in constant flux as political seasons and different administrations come and go—is actually beneficial. It is just so hard for conspiracies to grow very large before someone is going to talk to the media.

Still, that might be wishful thinking. A House IT aide with more than a decade of experience contacted for this book said it *is* possible that some staffers were getting kickbacks. "There is little oversight," he said. "Unless someone complains, it is doubtful investigators would step in to look over a congressman's books."

Either way, illegal things clearly did happen, yet Congress and much of the media simply didn't want to touch this criminal investigation linked to so many Democrats. Meanwhile, Congress began quietly moving to tighten its security as it tried to avoid media coverage. In November 2017, for example, the House held members-only "listening sessions" on the use of shared employees. The briefings focused on lawmakers' "use of shared employees to provide information technology services to member offices," according to a notice obtained by *Politico*.[57]

"The Committee on House Administration has been conducting an internal review on shared employees, specifically in the IT field. As a part of that process, the committee is hosting two identical bipartisan member-only listening sessions the week of November 13," committee spokeswoman Erin McCracken said in a statement.

Politico also downplayed the exposure by reporting: "Several hard-line conservatives and right-wing bloggers have seized on conspiracy theories related to the investigation, claiming that Awan had access to Wasserman Schultz's emails while she was chairwoman of the Democratic National Committee and that he, not Russia, was behind the leak of thousands of DNC emails during the election. The intelligence community, including the CIA and FBI, has said conclusively that Russia was behind the hacks as part of its widespread attempt to influence the 2016 election."

That's an opinionated and declarative statement from a publication that knows this is a complex story. Perhaps the mainstream media were simply being defensive about their Russia-gave-us-Trump narrative as they defended Democrats caught up in this multifaceted scandal. Still, it's telling that this reporter and others refused to consider in print that it might be more complicated than simply a Russian hack that was given to WikiLeaks so the DNC's emails could influence voters. It is also interesting that the authenticity of the leaked DNC emails has never been seriously questioned even by those who saw their emails go public during a presidential campaign.

Many in the media and the establishment don't seem to want to complicate the narrative with a healthy dose of investigative journalism or with hard questions, as new revelations could weaken or add nuance to the storyline so many in the Washington press corps have been repeating.

They even set out to debunk reports that the DNC hack actually might have been done by a staffer downloading the data, perhaps because that would implicate someone at the DNC or at least show that DNC procedures and oversight were at fault. This made news in right-leaning news outlets after a blogger who calls himself "the Forensicator" looked at the download times, which can be seen in the metadata of documents released by the hacker accused of being a Russian agent, known as Guccifer 2.0 (if indeed this is one person). The Forensicator saw that metadata indicates the files were downloaded at a speed of more than twenty megabytes per second, which is much too fast for most US-based internet speeds, though some large corporations and cloud networks might accomplish that download speed. (The DNC refused to say what its download speed was.)[58] Because of this, the Forensicator determined the documents could not have been copied over the internet. This would mean that someone with physical access to the network would have copied them in person to, say, a flash drive.

"This theory assumes that the hacker downloaded the files to a computer and then leaked it from that computer," Rich Barger, director of security research at Splunk, a San Francisco–based corporation that produces software for searching, monitoring, and analyzing machine-generated big data, told *The Hill*.[59] Barger's point is the files could have been copied multiple times, thereby creating new time stamps. Also, metadata can be altered, especially by sophisticated intelligence agencies like the Russians have.

Even so, weeks after this article from *The Hill* came out, and in a break from other left-leaning publications, *The Nation* questioned the Democrats' Russia-did-it narrative. In September 2017, the magazine published an article titled "A New Report Raises Big Questions About Last Year's DNC Hack."[60] This 4,500-word article by Patrick Lawrence, a longtime contributor to *The Nation*, generated loads of criticism from the Left. This position, however, isn't shocking, as *The Nation* endorsed Bernie Sanders for president in 2016, not Hillary Clinton.[61]

Still, many Democrats treated it as heresy to the shared orthodoxy that president Donald J. Trump's campaign colluded with the Russians. The backlash from liberals who'd mostly been fed one storyline by left-leaning publications and cable channels was so strong *The Nation* later added an editor's note to the top of the article:

> For more than 150 years, *The Nation* has been committed to fearless, independent journalism. We have a long history of seeking alternative views and taking unpopular stances. We believe it is important to challenge questionable conventional wisdom and to foster debate—not police it. Focusing on unreported or inadequately reported issues of major importance and raising questions

that are not being asked have always been a central part of our work.

This journalistic mission led *The Nation* to be troubled by the paucity of serious public scrutiny of the January 2017 intelligence-community assessment (ICA) on purported Russian interference in our 2016 presidential election, which reflects the judgment of the CIA, the FBI, and the NSA. That report concluded that Russian President Vladimir Putin personally ordered the hacking of the DNC and the dissemination of e-mails from key staffers via WikiLeaks, in order to damage Hillary Clinton's candidacy. This official intelligence assessment has since led to what some call "Russiagate," with charges and investigations of alleged collusion with the Kremlin, and, in turn, to what is now a major American domestic political crisis and an increasingly perilous state of US-Russia relations. To this day, however, the intelligence agencies that released this assessment have failed to provide the American people with any actual evidence substantiating their claims about how the DNC material was obtained or by whom. Astonishingly and often overlooked, the authors of the declassified ICA themselves admit that their "judgments are not intended to imply that we have proof that shows something to be a fact."

The Nation's article mostly drew on a report prepared by Veteran Intelligence Professionals for Sanity (VIPS), a group of former officers (mostly analysts) from the US intelligence community. VIPS was formed in 2003 in response to how the Bush administration characterized US national intelligence information as it marched toward the invasion of Iraq. This had won the group a lot of praise from the Left.

In this recent report, however, VIPS argued that the theft of the DNC emails wasn't a hack but was an inside leak that didn't involve Russia.

"Key among the findings of the independent forensic investigations is the conclusion that the DNC data was copied onto a storage device at a speed that far exceeds an Internet capability for a remote hack. Of equal importance, the forensics show that the copying was performed on the East Coast of the US. Thus far, mainstream media have ignored the findings of these independent studies.... VIPS member William Binney, a former Technical Director at the National Security Agency, and other senior NSA 'alumni' in VIPS attest to the professionalism of the independent forensic findings," said the VIPS report.[62]

VIPS even called out those in US intelligence agencies that said the Russians were behind the leak: "The recent forensic studies fill in a critical gap. Why the FBI neglected to perform any independent forensics on the original 'Guccifer 2.0' material remains a mystery—as does the lack of any sign that the 'hand-picked analysts' from the FBI, CIA, and NSA who wrote the 'Intelligence Community Assessment' dated January 6, 2017, gave any attention to forensics."

The Nation's editor, Katrina vanden Heuvel, summed it up by saying, "Despite all the media coverage taking the veracity of the ICA assessment for granted, even now we have only the uncorroborated assertion of intelligence officials to go on." Indeed, this was noticed by *The New York Times*' Scott Shane, who wrote the day the report appeared: "What is missing from the public report is...hard evidence to back up the agencies' claims that the Russian government engineered the election attack.... Instead, the message from the agencies essentially amounts to 'trust us.'"

In this case, *The Nation* is adhering to the Vietnam-era liberal belief that you can't just trust the government, an American cynicism more often found today on the Right. Meanwhile, the establishment Left mostly ignored the report from VIPS.

This isn't to say that Imran Awan or anyone from his crew had anything to do with the DNC leaks. As this was going to print, there was no evidence he had. But it should also be noted that, despite what the mainstream media has pushed, it also can't be ruled out that

Imran leaked the thousands of emails, many of which had attached documents. Imran was Representative Wasserman Schultz's IT person at the time this data got out, and this occurred before Wasserman Schultz was ousted from her lead role at the DNC. For reasons that aren't yet clear, Imran also copied emails and other data from dozens of congressmen to a server and Dropbox account he had control over, so it would seem to fit a pattern.

Actually, after Imran and his very well-paid but unqualified team of IT administrators were banned from the House network, several big developments moved this story further into the realm of a plot for a Hollywood spy thriller.

CHAPTER 2

THE "REPDWS" LAPTOP

*I think you're violating the rules when you conduct
your business that way, and you should expect that
there will be consequences.*

—Rep. Debbie Wasserman Schultz to
Capitol Hill police chief Matthew R. Verderosa[1]

On the night of April 6, 2017, Capitol Police found a bag left on the
second floor of the Rayburn House Office Building. The small backpack sat in what was once a phone booth. In this post-9/11 age of
terrorism, an abandoned bag in any public place, let alone a building
filled with the offices of US congressmen, must be taken seriously.
Capitol Police grabbed the bag.

When Capitol Police searched the bag, they found a laptop, a pho-
tocopy of Imran Awan's congressional ID, a notebook, and letters to
US attorneys. They also soon found that the laptop had the username
"RepDWS" (an abbreviation for "Rep. Debbie Wasserman Schultz").

A police report obtained by the *Daily Caller* said:

> On 4/6/2017 at 0021 hours, with the building
> closed to the public, AOC [Architect of the Capitol]

informed USCP [Capitol Police] Rayburn offices of an unattended bag in the phone booth on the 2nd floor. The officer received the open-contents visible bag and prepared a found property report. While reviewing the inventory of the bag contents, the officer found

#1 a Pakistani ID card with the name Mohommed Ashraf Awan

#2 a copy – not original – of a driver's license with name Imran Awan

#3 a copy (front and back) of his congressional ID

#4 an Apple laptop with the homescreen initials 'RepDWS'

#5 composition notebooks with notes handwritten saying 'attorney client privilege' and possibly discussing case details below

#6 loose letters addressed to US Attorney of DC discussing the apparent owner of the bag being investigated. Approximately 3–4 months ago officer was requested by SAA as police presence of 4 individuals being interviewed, including the bag owner. It is unknown to the officer whether he is still employed.

The bag was found just over two months after Imran had been banned by Capitol Police from Congress's network. Imran's attorney, Chris Gowen, would later say in court that the bag was accidentally left in that cubbyhole in the congressional building as Imran tried to get a better cell phone signal. Gowen declined to say, later when asked, what Imran was doing with a bag with a computer and letters to US attorneys in it in a congressional building near midnight.

This is especially odd behavior for someone who was under investigation by Capitol Police. Stranger still is the fact that Rep. Debbie Wasserman Schultz's office is in the Longworth House Office Building, while this bag was found in the Rayburn building. Since every congressman except Representative Wasserman Schultz had already fired Imran, what was he doing in the Rayburn building in the middle of the night?

Oddly, a letter from US Attorney Channing D. Phillips sent to Aaron Marr Page, one of Imran's attorneys with Gowen Rhoades Winograd & Silva PLLC, in the discovery phase of this case in August 2017 states that the bag was found in the Longworth building. This appears to be a mistake, as the official Capitol Police report says it was found in Rayburn.

Re: *U.S. v. Imran Awan*, 17-CR-161

Dear Mr. Page:

Enclosed please find a forensic image of the hard drive, which was recovered from the Longworth House Office Building on April 6, 2017, and a forensic image of the laptop computer, which was seized from your client at the time of his arrest. Also enclosed please find copies of materials from the notebook and laptop bag, which also were recovered from the Longworth House Office Building on April 6, 2017. Please let us know if you have any questions or concerns.

Sincerely,

CHANNING D. PHILLIPS
United States Attorney

Reproduction

Leaving important items in such a place accidentally is unlikely, says Rep. Louie Gohmert, a former prosecutor and member of the House Judiciary Committee. "Imran Awan is a calculating person who made great efforts to cover his tracks, both electronically and physically," said Representative Gohmert. "Placing that laptop with his personal documents, which may well incriminate him, those he worked for, or both, in the dead of night in a House office building, was a deliberate act by a cunning suspect, and it needs to be investigated."[2]

But then, was he even in Rayburn that night? Could an enemy of Imran, or perhaps an unhappy person from his team, have placed the bag in Rayburn? At the time Imran was still employed by Representative Wasserman Schultz, while all the other people on the team he recruited had been fired. When family members intermingle money the way the Awans did, there is apt to be some bad blood.

We don't know what was on the laptop or what the letters to the US attorneys say, but we do know that Wasserman Schultz wants the computer back so badly she actually threatened the Capitol Police chief with "consequences" in a public hearing if the computer being held as evidence wasn't promptly returned.

Capitol Police told her they'd confiscated the laptop and other items as evidence in their ongoing investigation into the Awans and their associates. That this evidence would be held as long as the investigation continues should be obvious to anyone; actually, leaving it there ensured the bag and its contents would be treated as evidence. That much must have been clear to Imran or whoever left the bag in the congressional building that night.

With the computer and letters in the bag left in the cubbyhole, according to Chris Gowen, was also a notebook that had "attorney client privilege" written in or on it. Gowen would later use this as a reason in court to ask that the notebook and laptop be given back to Imran, saying it was "protected by attorney-client privilege."

In an October 2017 court hearing, Gowen told the judge: "We do expect, there being an attorney-client privilege issue in this case... What occurred is a backpack from my client was found, he was trying to get a better signal, there was a note that said attorney-client privilege, and a hard drive. We feel very strongly about this."

Just how a handwritten note saying "attorney client privilege" could be construed to cover a hard drive, rather than the pages of the notebook it was written on, is unclear. Could an accused person further expand attorney-client privilege by telling police officers who've come to his door with a search warrant, "Sorry, my home is protected by attorney-client privilege; see, I wrote it right there on the front door"? Of course not. Attorney-client privilege only protects private client communications made to a lawyer for the purpose of obtaining legal advice. Just because someone was to, say, show bank records to their attorney doesn't mean that those records would then be protected by attorney-client privilege—only the advice the attorney gives would be.

Another part of the problem with the argument this computer is protected from the authorities by attorney-client privilege is because it's labeled "RepDWS," which would make it Representative Wasserman Schultz's property.

A complex set of rules does surround a congressman's property. Wasserman Schultz used this fact to try to get the evidence out of the hands of investigators, but even her statements with regard to who owned the computer changed as the investigation went on. To make her case, Wasserman Schultz hired an outside attorney, Bill Pittard, to argue that police and prosecutors should not be allowed to keep or look at the laptop because it is loaded with sensitive legislative information, which, Pittard argued, invokes the Constitution's "Speech or Debate Clause" that protects the information from the authorities.

Pittard, a partner with KaiserDillon PLLC, is a former acting general counsel for the US House of Representatives. Hiring an outside counsel, one with internal experience in Congress, to argue the Constitution's Speech or Debate Clause on behalf of Wasserman Schultz is unusual, as the acting general counsel of the House offers such opinions on speech and debate issues free of charge.

This constitutional protection has been upheld in court. Essentially, members of Congress have immunity for their legislative acts under Article I, Section 6, clause 1, of the Constitution, which provides that members of Congress "shall in all Cases, except Treason, Felony and Breach of the Peace, be privileged from Arrest during their attendance at the Session of their Respective Houses, and in going to and from the same; and for any Speech or Debate in either House, they shall not be questioned in any other Place."

The intended purpose of the Speech or Debate Clause is to prevent a president or other official in the executive branch from having members of Congress arrested or detained, actions that could be used to prevent them from voting a certain way or otherwise taking actions a president might not like.

There is strong legal ground protecting a member of Congress's computers, files, and more, especially when the records are in a congressional building. In 2006 this clause was even used to protect a member of Congress who would, without evidence initially seized from his office in the Rayburn House Office Building, later be convicted of bribery, racketeering, and money laundering.

In that case the FBI had raided the office of Rep. William J. Jefferson (D-LA) in the Rayburn building. The FBI raid ignited a bipartisan uproar among many of the 435 members of Congress. At the time, quite a few congressmen cited the Speech or Debate Clause, which had been used in 1971 to protect Sen. Mike Gravel (D-AK) as he moved copies of the Pentagon Papers in two suitcases into his Senate office.

Representative Jefferson challenged the raid as a violation of the speech and debate clause and in 2007, in *United States v. Rayburn House Office Building*, the US Court of Appeals for the District of Columbia Circuit unanimously ruled that the FBI's search was unconstitutional and ordered the bureau to return the privileged documents it had seized in the raid.

The trouble for Representative Wasserman Schultz is the computer wasn't seized from her office as part of a raid; it was found abandoned in a cubbyhole that was once a phone booth. Also, it hasn't been clearly established that the laptop is her property; it was seized as part of an investigation into her IT aide.

When asked about this, David Damron, spokesperson for Representative Wasserman Schultz, wouldn't clarify why Wasserman Schultz said the laptop was hers or how she'd lost it. He also wouldn't say why Wasserman Schultz later said the computer was Imran's or, when the fact that it had the username "RepDWS" rather than

Imran's username came out, why she then asked for it back under the premise it was actually her laptop.

Typically, when stories change like this, investigators put on pressure, as they know the person is likely lying. But this is a sensitive case having to do with dozens of congressmen, possible cybersecurity breaches involving members of Congress and their staffs, and much more.

Still, this should have prompted Capitol Police to ask more questions, as they had banned Imran from the House network on February 2, 2017. This would mean that Representative Wasserman Schultz was also prohibited from allowing Imran to touch anything having to do with the House network after February 2. If there is anything on the laptop showing that Imran was still able to access Wasserman Schultz's official emails or other data, then charges or an ethics complaint could be filed against both Imran and Wasserman Schultz.

Before this laptop was left in a congressional office building, and after Imran and the rest of his crew were prohibited from logging on to the House network, Representative Wasserman Schultz actually went out of her way to add Imran's wife, Hina Alvi, to her payroll in a newly created position as a second IT aide. Though Hina Alvi also couldn't go on Congress's network after February 2, 2017, Wasserman Schultz thought she should be paid with public money so she could advise her office on its computer system.

But then, in March 2017, about a month before the laptop was found, Hina Alvi left the country for Pakistan with $12,400 in cash and her children. We know she had $12,400 in cash and a lot of bags because authorities stopped her at Dulles International Airport and searched her bags. Nevertheless, even though she was under an active congressional investigation and was carrying more currency than is allowed by law, for some reason they let her fly away to Pakistan.

Hina Alvi's departure from the country did cause Representative Wasserman Schultz to stop paying her, but the congresswoman nevertheless kept paying Imran with taxpayer money.

A Threat of "Consequences"

This would all go public on May 17, 2017, when Representative Wasserman Schultz used a budget hearing with the House chief administrative officer to demand the return of the laptop and to claim it wasn't her fault that her emails and other data, and perhaps many other congressmen's data, was being backed up by Imran to a Dropbox account even though this is against House rules.[3]

"I am more than happy to admit that I use Dropbox," Wasserman Schultz said. "I have used it for years and years and years. It is not blocked. I am fully able to use it."

She also asked, "So members are not supposed to be using Dropbox?"

"Not according to the policy," said John Ramsey, the House's information security officer at the appropriations hearing.

Wasserman Shultz would also say, "So there is a vulnerability in our network in spite of the fact that you say that you've taken steps to address it. And there is not enough of a—of a policy that—that applies across the board. And you need to make sure that you tighten up your rules and policies so that you can really take and assure us that you take seriously protecting our network."

Administrators then informed her they had clearly communicated the House rules to IT aides. But instead of faulting Imran for not following these rules or passing them on to her or her chief of staff, Wasserman Schultz lashed out at the House for "just lobbing email into a tech person's in-box."

This should concern investigators, as several sources say the Awans' large-scale use of Dropbox was not some nonchalant use of a popular data-transfer site. They say Imran was clearly moving huge amounts of data off-site and out of the control of House authorities, though they don't know why.

During this same hearing, Wasserman Schultz threatened Capitol Police chief Matthew R. Verderosa with "consequences" if he didn't return the laptop that had been confiscated as part of the investigation.

"My understanding is the Capitol Police is not able to confiscate members' equipment when the member is not under investigation," Wasserman Schultz said in the police budget hearing of the House Committee on Appropriations' Legislative Branch Subcommittee.

"We can't return the equipment," Chief Verderosa replied.

"I think you're violating the rules when you conduct your business that way, and you should expect that there will be consequences," said Wasserman Schultz.

As one of eight members of the Committee on Appropriations' Subcommittee on the Legislative Branch, Representative Wasserman Schultz was partially in charge of the budget for the police force investigating Imran. Still, to be fair, it is unclear if Wasserman Schultz was referring to Capitol Police's budget when she made the threat. Of course, if her threat of "consequences" didn't pertain to Capitol Police's budget, it is also unclear just what she was referring to.

This odd exchange actually went on for about three minutes. Wasserman Schultz repeatedly tried to extract a promise from the chief that he would return evidence (the laptop) that was being used to build an active case.

"If a member loses equipment and it is found by your staff and identified as that member's equipment and the member is not associated with any case, it is supposed to be returned. Yes or no?" she said.

She was then told this was "an ongoing investigation," but she continued to press.

At this May 17, 2017, appropriations hearing, Representative Wasserman Shultz even tried to find out how much Capitol Police might know about her internet usage, asking, "Are members monitored?"[4]

"If a member is using an application outside of the House infrastructure and the protection of the…[of] our cybersecurity network, they're in violation of House policy?" she asked John Ramsey, the House's information security officer at the appropriations hearing.

"Of the House Policy 17, yes ma'am," Ramsey said.

Ramsey would also explain that his office communicates IT policy by notifying the IT personnel who work for congressional committees and congressmen.

"When the policy came out, ma'am, we had sent some targeted communications out to the various IT systems administrators that service...the members," Ramsey said.

So then, did Imran withhold information from his boss? Did Representative Wasserman Schultz violate policies because she was counting on Imran to tell her? If so, then the fox wasn't just watching the henhouse, but the farmer was actually checking in with the fox to see how the chickens were getting on.

Still, this doesn't appear to be quite right, as Wasserman Schultz should have been angry that her employee misled her. She should have at least discreetly fired Imran at this point. But instead, she would keep him on the payroll for months as she defended him and accused those writing about this investigation of anti-Muslim bigotry.

Actually, instead of having any of the normal reactions that a boss would have when discovering an employee has gone rogue, Representative Wasserman Schultz asked, "Wouldn't you think that you would have a policy where you inform every single member and that we actually have a meeting with each member's tech person so that you can inform them exactly what the rules are, what is allowable, what is not allowable?"

Chief administrative officer Phil Kiko then told her that "we do inform every IT person, IT administrator in every congressional office. If that's not enough..."

Actually, if Wasserman Schultz is right about one thing, it's that only telling the IT person is not nearly enough. The chief of staff at a minimum should also be in the loop just to prevent the IT person from again being the fox watching the henhouse. Even members of Congress shouldn't be this idiotic, as they are ripe for insiders to copy data and sell it to a foreign government or even to a corporation interested in a certain piece of legislation being passed or killed.

But Representative Wasserman Schultz didn't stop there. In that same May 17 hearing, she actually complained that congressmen don't have the ability to really put pressure on the chief of the Capitol Police since the chief reports to an independent board. Perhaps she was unhappy that the chief of the Capitol Police doesn't report to the

House Committee on Appropriations' legislative subcommittee, so she could really put her thumb on him.

"We have had jurisdictional issues and a challenging time conducting oversight because of the structure of the Capitol Police Board.... I'd like to know, Sergeant, if you think that we should be looking at restructuring the way the board makes decisions so that we can establish a more direct line of accountability," Wasserman Schultz said.

Many would note this exchange was particularly combative for an appropriations meeting, which is typically even more boring than C-SPAN coverage of a Monday morning on the House floor.

Representative Wasserman Schultz's outlandish conduct during the hearing even brought criticism from her 2016 primary opponent.

"We demand that Wasserman Schultz recuse herself from the House Committee on Appropriations' Legislative Branch Subcommittee on any matter dealing with the Capitol Police budget. She uses her position on this subcommittee to threaten the chief of the US Capitol Police," said Tim Canova, who ran against her in 2016 in the Democratic primary for the House seat she occupies, in a Facebook post.[5]

Canova, a Democrat, also said, "[A]s long as Wasserman Schultz is in public life, the Democratic Party will be dragged down."

Nevertheless, the Media Looked Away

Part of the reason the media has ignored this scandal, even after Representative Wasserman Schultz threatened the chief of Capitol Police with "consequences," is that more than three dozen House Democrats who'd employed Imran and his overpaid associates either weren't commenting or were downplaying the importance of the case.

But then, if forty, or even just a few Republican members of Congress had employed and paid millions of taxpayers' dollars in exorbitant salaries to a group of IT people Capitol Police were forced to toss off the official congressional system for alleged fraud, theft, cybersecurity breaches, and more, it would be hard to imagine the Washington media not chasing the story.

This, after all, is the kind of investigation journalists daydream about when they watch the 1976 film *All the President's Men* and imagine themselves as either Dustin Hoffman or Robert Redford meeting Deep Throat in the dim light of an underground parking garage. This is a rare story that offers a glimpse right into the wretched and stinking inner workings of a self-righteous, convulsing, blob-like mass known as a national political party. There is an element of Orson Welles's dark 1941 film *Citizen Kane* in the political intrigues and of the party machine exposed. There is fraud, theft, corruption, behind-the-scenes political machinations, international intrigue, Page Six-style spectacles we haven't gotten to yet, and a cover-up underway to protect Washington power all rolled into this story. This is hardly just some trifling case of bank fraud, with which Imran Awan and Hina Alvi Awan would later be charged.

The thing is, when a revealing, if at times tabloid-style drama happens to be harmful to the party that a majority of journalists root for—and that their publications back—sure, they might reel back in horror for a news cycle, but they will soon start to shape a narrative to heal the very public wound. Nothing to see here, folks, just some right-wing conspiracy blowing up like a fireworks factory on Capitol Hill, that's all.

The *Washington Post* would say the story "has attracted unfounded conspiracy theories and intrigue" from "far-right news organizations."[6] *Politico* reported, "Several hardline conservatives and right-wing bloggers have seized on conspiracy theories related to the investigation."[7] *Slate* said, "[M]any of the sensational details...have been cooked up by conservative conspiracy-mongers."[8]

Some bloggers on the Right have certainly lobbed unsubstantiated theories at this case, just as some in the Left's blogosphere say some outlandish things about president Donald J. Trump. But just because someone postulates in their blog that Rep. Debbie Wasserman Schultz must be having an affair with Imran Awan to try to explain why she has been extraordinarily loyal to him (hardly a normal characteristic for a politician and not a trait Wasserman Schultz is known for) doesn't invalidate the facts.

Also, part of the reason these bloggers and others are tossing out theories is because the media has shown little interest in reporting this story. If the mainstream media had done just a little digging flavored with just a hint of open-minded honesty, then more of the facts would be out there, taking the hot air out of the unsubstantiated intrigue.

By not doing their jobs, these journalists are partly responsible for how this story is being treated.

Nevertheless, instead of looking into this, many in the media have simply sided with Imran's attorney, Chris Gowen, a man who'd previously worked in Bill Clinton's administration and who worked on Hillary Clinton's 2008 campaign for president.[9] But then, none of this is new, as the mainstream media often treats a story that's unfavorable to Democrats in this way in the hopes the story will shrivel and die outside of their light. This is also what they did with the Obama administration's gunrunning scandal known as Operation Fast and Furious.

In that case, the Department of Justice, via the Bureau of Alcohol, Tobacco, Firearms, and Explosives (ATF), told gun store owners to sell known bad guys all the guns they wanted. The ATF then failed to track and/or confiscate the guns before they slipped south into the arsenals of Mexican drug cartels. Two of those guns were later used to murder a US Border Patrol agent in December 2010, and many more have been used to murder Mexicans. Even all that wasn't juicy enough for most journalists who vote for Democrats to pursue.

Actually, how the media treated Operation Fast and Furious during the Obama administration is a very helpful way to understand how they are handling this case involving a rogue team of IT people and dozens of Democrats in the House of Representatives.

The clearest way to see this duplicity from the media is to highlight an exception, and Sharyl Attkisson was a great big exception—so startling an exception that the Obama administration repeatedly contacted her bosses in an effort to silence her.

Attkisson was an investigative correspondent in CBS News' Washington bureau. She also substituted as anchor for the *CBS Evening News*. She resigned from CBS News on March 10, 2014, after twenty-one years with the network, when it became clear CBS was stonewalling her investigation into the Obama administration's Operation Fast and Furious.

In February 2011, a letter was sent anonymously to Attkisson's producer at CBS News. In the envelope was a copy of a letter Sen. Charles Grassley (R-IA) had sent to ATF acting director Kenneth E. Melson. Grassley wanted information about the ATF-sanctioned sale of hundreds of firearms to straw purchasers (people who can pass a background check and buy a gun or guns for someone who can't).

"The letter was so explicit I knew there was something big going on. I could tell Grassley had whistleblowers," said Attkisson.

She pursued the story. Over the next year and more, her reporting exposed the government-overseen gunrunning operation and the massive cover-up in progress to hide it. As she reported on the scandal, however, Attkisson said, "CBS was less and less inclined to run stories on Fast and Furious."[10]

As she continued to interview ATF agents-turned-whistleblowers and to pursue other stories that turned out to be critical of the Obama administration, she noticed her reports were not making it on air. She was quietly being shunned.

Attkisson had made a career of getting to the bottom of big stories. In 2000 she received an Investigative Reporters and Editors Finalist award for "Dangerous Drugs in 2000." In 2001 she received an Emmy Award nomination for "Firestone Tire Fiasco" from the National Academy of Television Arts and Sciences. In 2008 she made headlines by saying a claim by Hillary Clinton that she had dodged sniper fire in Bosnia wasn't true—Attkisson had been one of the media members on the trip. In 2010 she received an Emmy Award nomination for her investigation into a waste of tax dollars. In 2012 Accuracy in Media gave her an Investigative Reporting Award for her reporting on Fast and Furious. In June 2012 her investigative reporting on Fast and Furious also won CBS Evening News the Radio and Television News Directors Association's National Edward R. Murrow Award for Excellence in Video Investigative Reporting. The accomplishments go on, but you get the point.

Meanwhile, as Attkisson investigated Fast and Furious, she says, "Obama officials were calling my bosses constantly, as well as emailing them—and calling and emailing me." Emails would later show they were trying to get her under "control."

Records obtained via a lawsuit filed by Judicial Watch—after the Department of Justice ignored a Freedom of Information Act request—show that the DOJ's spokesperson at the time, Tracy Schmaler, discussed ways to keep the press from reporting on Operation Fast and Furious with White House deputy press secretary Eric Schultz on October 4, 2011.

Schmaler wrote, "I've talked to *NYT*, NBC and NPR—gave them all this. NBC not likely to go. Still waiting on other two."

Judicial Watch notes that the talking points Schmaler sent to the news outlets (the "all this") were redacted (blacked out) in the court-ordered release. How can talking points sent to media outlets be shielded by a president's executive privilege?

In the email exchange, Schultz then asked Schmaler: "Any way we can fix Fox?"

Schmaler replied, "No stories...From *NYT*, *AP*, *Reuters*, *WaPo*, NBC, Bloomberg...I'm also calling Sharryl's editor and reaching out to Scheiffer. She's out of control."

Schultz said, "Good. Her piece was really bad for AG [the attorney general]. Why do you think nobody else wrote? Were they not fed the docs?"[11]

This one email chain implicates both the Obama White House and the DOJ. They were working to undermine a congressional investigation and to suppress media reports that might be critical of the Obama administration—and much of the media was going along with them.

Judicial Watch also noted the released "documents show that Obama made the extraordinary assertion of executive privilege over emails between Eric Holder and his wife, Sharon Malone. The emails show that Holder sent his spouse internal DOJ emails about Fast and Furious developments. There is nothing that would have been covered by executive privilege in these or other key records that show Barack

Obama abused his power to keep them secret during his reelection campaign up until now."

Of course, the "Sharryl" the DOJ spokesperson was referring to is Sharyl Attkisson. When asked if she was surprised her name had been mentioned in this way or that Obama administration officials had called her employers, Attkisson told me, "No. I'm sure my name is mentioned in hundreds of emails between Obama administration officials."

This led me to wonder whether the exchange printed above was only released because Sharyl's name was misspelled, as it wouldn't have turned up in a basic word search. Sharyl laughed and said, "Probably."

After her departure from CBS, Attkisson would write and publish *Stonewalled: My Fight for Truth Against the Forces of Obstruction, Intimidation, and Harassment in Obama's Washington*, in which she details the Obama administration's efforts to monitor and harass journalists. She also indicts much of the media for smothering investigative journalism as they favor one political party.

Attkisson even found that her computers had been hacked. Her computers, she says, were literally turning themselves on and off at night. When a confidential source offered to have her CBS laptop examined by a well-placed forensics expert, the examination revealed it had been hacked by a sophisticated party that used software proprietary to a government agency. The examination showed the intruders had also gotten into the CBS system. Attkisson reported this to CBS, and the corporation hired its own computer forensics firm, which confirmed that her CBS laptop and her personal Apple desktop had been subject to remote intrusions. Later, Attkisson also hired private computer forensic experts who, she says, provided a third confirmation of remote intrusions and found evidence of government involvement.

Still, all that would receive very little coverage from much of the media.

After becoming frustrated that her investigative journalism wasn't making it to the public, and with some of her sources worrying about being found out by eavesdropping Obama administration officials, she decided it was time to leave CBS.

Attkisson said, "Since publishing my book *Stonewalled*, I've had a lot of journalists contact me to say 'thank you' and to tell me about similar challenges they have faced in getting original and investigative reporting published."

When asked if she would tell today's journalism students to challenge authority the way she has, Attkisson said, "It's difficult to advise journalism students to argue with their future bosses over story decisions because it might cost them their careers. But they should never agree to do anything that is dishonest or factually incorrect."

Attkisson was reluctant to label CBS as a propaganda arm for Democrats. However, she did say there was a culture at CBS when she worked there, and at other mainstream news outlets, that has been reluctant to be critical of Democrats, just as they are behaving in this case involving Rep. Debbie Wasserman Schultz and dozens of other House Democrats.

One example Attkisson cited in her book is how CBS sat on a video that would have harmed Barack Obama during a key point in the 2012 presidential election. During the second debate, Mitt Romney and Obama sparred over when Obama first had called the coordinated Benghazi attacks "terrorism." Obama claimed he had called the attacks terrorism in a Rose Garden speech the day after they occurred, but a video interview recorded that same day with CBS's Steve Kroft shows that Obama agreed when Kroft contended Obama had not called the Benghazi attacks terrorism. In that interview, Obama said the reason he did not call them acts of terror was because "it was too early to tell." Instead of running that video when it was very newsworthy, CBS acted as if the video didn't exist.

Certainly, decisions like this one don't involve every person at a news organization—CBS hardly called all its reporters and producers together to vote on whether to make the video public—but it clearly shows management was rooting for a certain team and that they were willing to cheat to win.

Meanwhile, what makes marginalizing people like Attkisson particularly problematic is that few journalists outside of the big media outlets today have the resources to back up FOIA requests with lawsuits. This is why when Attkisson left CBS she turned to Judicial Watch, which has had a great deal of success suing the government for FOIA violations. Judicial Watch did file FOIA requests and lawsuits on Attkisson's behalf and, as this was being written, had filed a few to see what really happened with Imran Awan and this scandal involving Rep. Debbie Wasserman Schultz and dozens of other House Democrats.

When asked about this, Tom Fitton, president of Judicial Watch, said, "One of our strengths as an organization is that we continue to invest time and resources into investigations and litigation after the headlines fade.... We frequently must file lawsuits to get agencies to respond to FOIA requests. Unfortunately, there are no real penalties imposed upon agencies for refusing to comply with FOIA requests, so they are often ignored—until we file suit."

What Attkisson and Fitton are saying is that Washington, DC, is a place where, if journalists want to keep access to their sources and to get promotions from their publications, they'd better not be too critical of Democrats, especially those who are still in positions of power.

The culture and viewpoints of establishment journalists in Washington can be a hard thing for those who haven't waded into the swamp to fully comprehend.

When Stephen Hunter, a bestselling novelist and former movie critic for the *Washington Post* (he won a Pulitzer while at the *Post*), was asked to articulate how Washington journalists are shaped, he put it this way: "Reporters at places like the *Post* are trained to believe in consensus. They believe in accord and compromise. Individualism, to them, is akin to becoming an outlier, a person fallen from the inner circles of society. If they step away from the accepted ethos, they'll be shunned; they won't be promoted. This is often unsaid, but the pressure to conform is profound. Everything they're taught tells them to look for accepted values, to conform to the group, and that anything outside those norms must be shunned. Though as a group they're mostly well educated, they're also mostly looking inward. Reporters speak to each other more than anyone else. They reinforce each other's values and assure each other they're the smartest people in the room. So no, they are not going to pursue stories that go against the herd."[12]

In those Washington media circles, it is smart to be a liberal. Most universities don't give tenure to conservatives, and most of the big urban papers, as well as broadcast news outlets like NBC, ABC, CBS, and CNN, don't promote people who aren't blue to the core.

You can see this culture on display in the newspaper boxes along Washington's Pennsylvania Avenue and hear it broadcast on many of the cable news networks and see it repeated as a refrain on most of the Washington-based news websites.

Sure, to most Americans who visit Capitol Hill as tourists, Washington is an open, clean destination dotted with historic monuments and stately stone buildings, some with pillars and long white stone steps rising to power.

Part of the reason the nation's capital has this feel is that in 1910, the 61st Congress enacted a law that raised the overall building height limit to 130 feet, but restricted building heights to the width of the adjacent street or avenue plus 20 feet. Thus, a building facing a 90-foot-wide street can be only 110 feet tall, or about 13 stories. Washington, by this decree, was to stay a short city as other skylines rose into the clouds.

The height limit has allowed the Capitol Dome to remain iconic, even ostentatious, as it's actually spectacularly small for such a country as the United States of America. If buildings around it were allowed to grow as they have in New York or Chicago, we would hardly notice the Capitol Dome topped solemnly with the Statue of Freedom.

Tourists also notice that Washington's sidewalks and the halls of congressional buildings aren't even bustling, not like Manhattan's. Stop and look and you'll see young men in dark suits, black shoes, and white or blue shirts, with bright ties, and young women in business suits or dresses walking along large sidewalks between wide avenues. Mixed with them are the tourists in T-shirts and jeans or Dockers. Beneath the streets are underground walks and even a small underground train for members of Congress and their staffs to hurry from the congressional buildings to the Capitol Building for votes, so part of the hustle is hidden.

Still, Washington, in comparison to Manhattan, is a quiet town full of power and money and connections. It's a place of influence being sold and wielded in a way often completely detached from the real needs of the people. Washington lives at a subjective distance from the reality found on Main Street America. Washington is white paper and pageantry and ideology moving along on theory, power, ego, and connections, not the reality of rent, car payments, and profits versus losses.

Sure, Washington's facade is stately. The grass on Capitol Hill is green and cut often, and the trees are trimmed and the buildings are simple and refined. Washington is the clothes of a man, as Paris is the bright evening gown on a lady. This makes sense, as Washington walks like a man. It sticks its chin out like a man. It is stoical and juvenile like a man. It lives on power and stupidity and ego like a man. No one really understands Washington, as most men don't completely understand themselves. No one controls Washington—not the 435 members of the House or the 100 senators or the president and all his cabinet positions and other officials and certainly not the media. Washington is a manly thing, a living thing that can either be overfed and corpulent or starved to improve its bearing. It can't really be fundamentally changed, at least short of war. Like Wall Street, it is an uncontrollable, illogical, and proud thing that some ride and some are trampled by, but that most are just trying to get what they can from.

Washington, beneath its granite and marble facade, has a well-established culture guided by gentlemanly laws and norms. Like an old gentleman's code, everything is accepted that doesn't make a public spectacle or kick the status quo in the groin. As it is with an old-school gentleman, a chauvinist perhaps and an egotist certainly, it is easier to go along with Capitol Hill culture than to buck its unwritten rules. This is part of the reason why so many outsiders are baffled when a maverick, a real Mr. Smith Goes to Washington type, arrives in DC and quickly morphs into just another Washington politician, one earmark and altered position at a time.

Even a man like Rep. Ken Buck (R-CO), who only came to Congress in 2015 but who quickly wrote an appalled and important exposé on Congress and the political system called *Drain the Swamp*, feels the pressure to conform. He told me over lunch on Capitol Hill as I was doing research for this book that he didn't come to Washington with a lot of friends and he wasn't likely to leave with a lot of friends.

The friction Representative Buck feels has been very public as tea party Republicans/members of the Freedom Caucus in Congress run head on into establishment Republicans. Buck is a founding member of the Freedom Caucus. *USA Today* even opened a story on him by saying, "Ken Buck hasn't made a lot of friends in Washington as a founding member of the often unruly, ultra-conservative Freedom Caucus that's fond of challenging the party's leaders on Capitol Hill."[13]

Representative Buck detests Washington's "pay-to-play" system and said that the Republican establishment gives the plum committee assignments and leadership slots to lawmakers who raise a lot of money for the party. "The key thing for a member of Congress to get ahead is fundraising; meanwhile, the reality is that the people you are going to raise money from will want something [from Congress]," said Buck.

In his book, Representative Buck explains the dues congressmen are required to pay to the House Republican campaign committee to keep their seats on influential committees. For example, to keep his position as a member of the House Rules Committee—one of the five "A" committees, which also include Appropriations, Ways and Means, Financial Services, and Energy and Commerce—Buck says he must raise $450,000 over his two-year term for the GOP's House campaign arm. The chairman of an "A" committee must raise even more, about $1.2 million, he says. This is why "some members of Congress spend at least half their time fundraising," Buck says.

As he signed my copy of his book over lunch, Representative Buck said, "A lot of people leave Congress and then write a book about the awful system, but I think it's better to write a book while I'm here." When asked if there was anything he could do about the Washington culture that was then shielding criticism of the more than forty House Democrats who'd hired Imran Awan and his team of IT administrators, he said, "I'm working within the system because the only way to change the system is for the American people to know what's going on and to put pressure on Congress to change."

Representative Buck then instructed his staff to tell him how much they pay for IT support and to help however else they could to bring accountability and change. When asked why Republican leadership hasn't been very interested in going on the record with this story, he said, "Most congressmen don't want attention placed on their internal staffing positions."

Speaker of the House Paul Ryan did say in a news conference in Washington in March 2017 that US Capitol Police are getting "the kind of help they need from other sources" in the investigation of Imran Awan and his associates. He continued: "I won't speak to the nature of their investigation, but they're getting the kind of technical assistance they need to do that. This is under an active criminal investigation; their capabilities are pretty strong, but they're also able to go and get the kind of help they need from other sources."

After making that statement, Speaker Ryan stopped talking about the case. Ryan and others in Republican leadership didn't respond to media requests asking about what the House is doing to safeguard Congress's (and our) data from criminal activity, which the Awans certainly engaged in.

Many congressional sources have said that if the public gets outraged enough with how these IT administrators were able to draw salaries of just less than what congressmen make as they improperly accessed data from congressmen and their staffs, and allegedly stole tens of thousands of dollars of equipment, then the public just might demand change, and change could mean more scrutiny of the budgets and staffs for members of Congress. That would be a direct assault on their power. Other sources on Capitol Hill said the Democrats don't want this case to get attention for obvious reasons, but the Republican establishment is also skeptical of this investigation, as they see it as too conspiratorial to have their names connected to. For these reasons only a few Republicans, basically those in the Freedom Caucus or those known as "tea party Republicans," have been interested in this case.

Given this Washington culture, where accountability can be fleeting, money fungible, and the media mostly ignore scandals involving Democrats, Rep. Debbie Wasserman Schultz had good reason to believe she could simply ignore this scandal and do as she pleased. She has, after all, been playing this game for years, though lately she has been losing hand after hand as she bet on Hillary Clinton and Imran Awan.

Wasserman Schultz first entered Congress in 2005, winning what's known as a "safe" seat in the House. She won reelection easily again and again every two years. But then, before the 2016 election, an economist and law professor named Tim Canova gave her a serious challenge in the August 30, 2016, primary. Canova was actually endorsed by Sen. Bernie Sanders during a time when it had become clear that Representative Wasserman Schultz had played a part in rigging the DNC's nomination process against Sanders and for Hillary Clinton.

Weeks before the primary, on August 8, 2016, in the wake of the WikiLeaks DNC email disclosures, Canova filed a Federal Election Commission violations of regulations complaint against Wasserman Schultz that alleged "interference" with his campaign. The complaint said that on her behalf "the DNC paid a team of national, senior communications and political professionals significant sums of money for their consulting services and the Wasserman Schultz for Congress Campaign utilized these services free of charge."

A spokesman for Representative Wasserman Schultz said the complaint was without merit and that it was "based on stolen, cherry-picked information," but this kind of frontal attack on a Democrat in a safe seat by another Democrat runs counter to the Washington establishment culture. Wasserman Schultz was suddenly very weak, but nevertheless, media bias and the Washington media shielded enough of the criticism for her to survive.

Wasserman Schultz won her 2016 primary with 57 percent of the vote. Subsequently, in the general election, she defeated Republican candidate Joe Kaufman, tallying 56.7 percent of the vote to Kaufman's 40.5 percent. That's a big margin but actually incredibly close for her district, which is overweighed with Democrats and includes parts of Broward and Miami-Dade Counties, including parts of Fort Lauderdale, Miami, and Miami Beach. Anyone who has watched the map change color during a presidential election night knows commentators keep pointing out that big turnouts in these areas are what Democrats need to win Florida.

One of the biggest complaints by Bernie Sanders against Wasserman Schultz as she ran the DNC was that, under her leadership, the committee scheduled only six debates in the 2016 presidential primary. This was about half as many as in previous election cycles, and two of these debates were actually held on Saturday nights.

Incredibly, just weeks before Hillary Clinton and Sanders were slated to compete in the Iowa Caucuses, Wasserman Schultz went to war with the Sanders campaign by shutting down their access to the DNC's voter database.[14] This caused Sanders's campaign to sue the DNC in federal court for $600,000 per day of lost access.[15] CNN reported at that time that the "internal warfare exploded after the DNC cut off Sanders from the database and said the Vermont senator's presidential campaign exploited a software error to improperly access confidential voter information collected by Hillary Clinton's team.... The DNC database is a goldmine of information about voters and being blocked from it could complicate Sanders's outreach efforts."

We now know from Donna Brazile, who ran the DNC just after Wasserman Schultz was ousted after leaked emails showed she was rigging the game for Hillary, that the DNC at the time was basically controlled by the Hillary campaign.[16] As a result, it is hardly a surprise that the Clinton campaign at the time viewed the DNC's voter database as its own.

After they were locked out of the DNC's voter database, Sanders's campaign manager, Jeff Weaver, accused the DNC of unfairly undermining their campaign: "The DNC, in an inappropriate overreaction, has denied us access to our own data. In other words, the leadership of the Democratic National Committee is actively trying to undermine our campaign."

Pressure from Sanders's progressive base of voters would force Wasserman Schultz and the DNC to let the Sanders campaign back into the DNC's voter database, but not until after some damage was done.

Wasserman Schultz also defended the system of superdelegates the DNC used to ensure that Clinton would be the inevitable nominee.[17] She also quietly rescinded Obama's 2008 ban on donations to the DNC from corporate lobbyists and political action committees,[18] which paved the way for the Hillary Victory Fund—as later reported by *Politico*—to launder money to the Clinton campaign. She even hid the details of the DNC's agreement with the Clinton campaign, an agreement that allowed the Clinton camp to treat the DNC as a surrogate for its campaign against Sanders. Wasserman Schultz had her fingers in all of this, as Donna Brazile would point out in her 2017 book *Hacked*.

In an article promoting her book at *Politico*, Brazile blew up the mainstream media's narrative by writing:

> Before I called Bernie Sanders, I lit a candle in my living room and put on some gospel music. I wanted to center myself for what I knew would be an emotional phone call.
>
> I had promised Bernie when I took the helm of the Democratic National Committee after the convention that I would get to the bottom of whether Hillary Clinton's team had rigged the nomination process, as a cache of emails stolen by Russian hackers and posted online had suggested. I'd had my suspicions from the moment I walked in the door of the DNC a month or so earlier, based on the leaked emails. But who knew if some of them might have been forged? I needed to have solid proof, and so did Bernie.
>
> So I followed the money. My predecessor, Florida Rep. Debbie Wasserman Schultz, had not

been the most active chair in fundraising at a time when President Barack Obama's neglect had left the party in significant debt. As Hillary's campaign gained momentum, she resolved the party's debt and put it on a starvation diet. It had become dependent on her campaign for survival, for which she expected to wield control of its operations.

Debbie was not a good manager. She hadn't been very interested in controlling the party—she let Clinton's headquarters in Brooklyn do as it desired so she didn't have to inform the party officers how bad the situation was. How much control Brooklyn had and for how long was still something I had been trying to uncover for the last few weeks.

By September 7, the day I called Bernie, I had found my proof and it broke my heart.[19]

As they have done with the House Democrats' IT scandal, the media quickly moved to silence the messenger by attacking Brazile, even though she is one of their own, as they defended their narrative.

This fissure between the establishment and progressive wings of the Democratic Party has shaken it just as much as the Republican Party has been split open by tumultuous battles between its establishment and tea party factions. What's interesting with regard to Democrats is that their odd, perhaps at times illegal, and senseless mistakes with cybersecurity and IT support have exposed them and our election process to so much mayhem.

In a poignant example, in May 2016, MSNBC's Mika Brzezinski said Wasserman Schultz should step down as head of the DNC because of her bias against the Bernie Sanders campaign.[20] The 2016 DNC email leak would later reveal that Wasserman Schultz was so furious with the negative coverage, she emailed NBC's Chuck Todd to say this harsh treatment of her "must stop."[21] She described the coverage as the "LAST straw" and ordered the DNC's communications director to call MSNBC president Phil Griffin to demand an apology from Brzezinski.[22]

Like many Democrats, Representative Wasserman Schultz wasn't used to negative treatment from the mainstream media—Fox News, sure, but not MSNBC.

As Wasserman Schultz struggled to keep her post at the DNC, and as she worked to protect Hillary Clinton—a Clinton administration would surely have benefitted her—she had Imran Awan employed as her official IT person.

If Representative Wasserman Schultz was willing to ban the Sanders campaign from the DNC's voter database weeks before the Iowa Caucuses—even though a legal agreement between the Sanders campaign and the DNC stated that the DNC had to give ten days' notice before making any changes to access and, of course, despite the backlash that would surely come (and did) from Bernie's voters—then it's conceivable that Wasserman Schultz paid, and later protected, Imran so he could do other computer-related chicanery for her.

Though we don't know if Imran had full access to the DNC's servers, WikiLeaks-released emails show he did have password access to the iPhone and iPad used by Representative Wasserman Schultz while she was running the DNC.[23] He could have used either of these devices to log in to the DNC's servers—the same ones the DNC refused to give the FBI access to.

The *New York Post* said a "senior US official," who asked for his name not to be used, said investigators looking into what Imran Awan and his associates were up to "suspect that sensitive US government data—possibly including classified information—could have been compromised and may have been sold to hostile foreign governments that could use it to blackmail members of Congress or even put their lives at risk. 'This is a massive, massive scandal.'"[24]

Imran had access to the DNC, via Wasserman Schultz's devices, but it still isn't clear just how much data he was able to see and perhaps copy. We do know that around or during the period in which Wasserman Schultz ran the DNC (from May 4, 2011, to July 28, 2016), Imran was copying all the emails, calendars, and other data he and his team could vacuum up from the computer systems of the congressmen they worked for. And we know the data was being copied to an off-site server and possibly to a Dropbox account.

The taxpayers' dollars confiscated from Congress are "not the highest of our concerns," Rep. Steve King (R-IA) told *WND*. "The American people deserve to know the truth to this; it is a big deal. It's not just $6 or $7 million, $120,000 worth of equipment here or there. The biggest thing is that the brothers, Awan's wife, and friend all had access to the private emails and electronic communications of members of Congress and all their staff."[25]

Representative King said there's "no telling what they downloaded, what they know.... They've had access to all of the computers of about sixty Democratic House members. The access of that information would not have been limited. They would have had the passwords for all of those members of Congress."

Though Representative Wasserman Schultz says Imran didn't have access to any classified information, Representative King refutes the former DNC chair's claims. King points out that Democratic members of Congress who serve on intelligence committees would, by the sheer nature of their work, correspond about sensitive information.

"The argument is that there was no classified information that was compromised or breached—that's what they said about Hillary Clinton at first," he said. "Some of them—like Andre Carson served on the Select Committee on Intelligence—would have access to the highest level of classified information that we have in the United States Congress."

Representative King argued that the Democrats who employed Imran and his crew basically gave up highly classified material to people from Pakistan who "don't have allegiance to the United States."

King also said, "When we hire people to work in our office, I want to make sure I am looking them in the eye. I want to know whose doing what work and what they're going to get paid for that. That's our jobs to do that.

"Instead, they are funneling taxpayer dollars to people who, at a minimum, are not natural-born American citizens. If they're sending money to Pakistan and absconding to Pakistan, they don't have allegiance to the United States, either."

This story remained at a quiet roar within Washington circles until Imran Awan tried to flee the country.

CHAPTER 3

THE ARREST

After details of the investigation were reviewed with us, my office was provided no evidence to indicate that laws had been broken, which over time, raised troubling concerns about due process, fair treatment, and potential ethnic and religious profiling. Upon learning of his arrest, he was terminated.

—Official statement of Rep. Debbie
Wasserman Schultz in July 2017

Imran Awan had every reason to believe US Customs and Border Protection would let him board Qatar Airways Flight 708 from Dulles International Airport on July 24, 2017, to Doha, Qatar, so he could transfer to a connection to Lahore, Pakistan. After all, his wife, Hina Alvi Awan, had been detained before her flights to Lahore on March 5, 2017, but had been allowed to fly away. They let her go even though FBI special agent Brandon Merriman said he didn't "believe that Alvi [had] any intention [of] returning to the United States."[1]

Agent Merriman, along with other FBI agents and US Capitol Police officers, had detained Hina Alvi at Dulles International

Airport. Hina Alvi was with her three children who, Merriman says, he "later learned were abruptly taken out of school without notifying the Fairfax County Public School System."

Hina Alvi also "had numerous pieces of luggage with her, including cardboard boxes." Agent Merriman said, "A secondary search of those items revealed that the boxes contained household goods, clothing, and food items. US Customs and Border Protection (CBP) conducted a search of Alvi's bags immediately prior to her boarding the plane and located a total of twelve thousand four hundred dollars in US cash inside."

Federal law requires anyone carrying $10,000 or more in cash into or out of the United States to fill out paperwork declaring how much they are carrying and why. They must fill out a Report of International Transportation of Currency or Monetary Instruments and file it with CBP. If someone tries to smuggle $10,000 or more in cash without completing the form, they are committing a felony punishable by up to five years in prison. If they are attempting to smuggle this currency as they are committing some other crime (such as fraud, for instance), the penalty is up to ten years in prison.

The affidavit from the FBI doesn't say whether Hina Alvi had filed a CBP currency-transportation report. It is unlikely that she did, as the form requires the person traveling with the currency to say whose money they are carrying, how they obtained the funds, where the money is being taken, who is going to receive it, and more. Even if she lied on this form, the information would be very relevant to an investigation into bank fraud, which is what Hina Alvi and Imran Awan were indicted for. For these reasons, if she'd filled out the form, it would be very odd for it not to be referenced in the affidavit later used to indict her and her husband.

Nevertheless, the authorities opted not to detain her to give US attorneys the chance to prosecute her; they did this even though it seemed clear that Hina Alvi was not planning to return.

This must have made Imran think they'd likely let him do the same. He had purchased a return ticket to come back to the United States in about six months (in January 2018). Also, as no charges had yet been filed in the ongoing investigation, and given that he was still working as an IT aide for Rep. Debbie Wasserman Schultz, Imran must have thought he'd be able to flee the US justice system just as his wife had.

Imran nevertheless took precautions. According to assistant US attorney Michael Marando, Imran wiped his iPhone just before entering the security line into the airport. "Two phones were found on [Imran] when he was arrested at Dulles International," said Marando. "One of the phones had been wiped clean just a few hours before."

When this came up in court months later, Imran's attorney, Chris Gowen, tried to muddle these facts by saying, "Awan had recently bought the phone, so of course it didn't have any data on it."

But Marando was ready for that. He told the judge the FBI found the phone had been wiped on purpose. He explained that FBI computer-forensic experts had found a time stamp on the iPhone indicating it had been wiped at 6:30 p.m. on July 24, 2017,, just hours before Imran's flight. Imran had used a function on the iPhone allowing its owner to wipe it clean if he or she wishes to sell or dispose of the phone, a function that typically leaves a time stamp showing when it had been wiped.

Marando said Imran likely knew he'd be stopped and interrogated at the airport, just as his wife had been stopped and searched, so he wiped the phone to avoid giving prosecutors more evidence. He could have, for example, been hiding his contacts in Pakistan and elsewhere. His contacts in Pakistan alone would be very interesting to the FBI's Joint Terrorism Task Force, which at that time had been investigating Imran for about a year.

Since Hina Alvi and their children flew away in March to Pakistan, a country with a very unclear extradition treaty with the United States (the arrangement dates back to a previous agreement with the British when they controlled India and Pakistan), Special Agent Merriman had been interviewing tenants who'd rented homes from the Awans, bank officials, and others to build a case. When Imran was about to flee the country (Gowen says he informed the authorities that Imran was about to travel to Pakistan), Agent Merriman, who only became an agent in January 2016, worked with US attorneys to press a clear charge they had prepared: bank fraud.

When they need to, district attorneys (or in this case a US attorney) will often use a smaller charge to get an indictment so they can hold a suspect as law enforcement continues to investigate. This bank fraud charge had the air of that kind of hold on Imran Awan.

Agent Merriman said his principal duties include "the investigation of criminal allegations of bribery and corruption involving public officials, mail fraud, wire fraud, and government fraud. I have had both training and experience in the investigation of crimes involving fraud and have worked with other FBI agents who have such experience...who have provided me with additional information about such crimes." Being so new to the agency, he would certainly need oversight of more veteran agents.

Agent Merriman put Imran in handcuffs and took his passports away—both Imran and Hina Alvi have passports from the United States and Pakistan. Imran was taken from the airport and put in a holding cell. He would be arraigned the next day.

By this time, Luke Rosiak, a reporter for the *Daily Caller*, had been writing about this case for some time. A few other publications had printed stories when Imran and his team were tossed off the US House of Representatives computer network on February 2, 2017. But most publications and networks either didn't cover this deep and evolving cyber scandal or quickly let it fade away. That changed when Imran was arrested. Now, the mainstream media would at least have to address the case, even if this investigation involving theft of tens of thousands of dollars of equipment, cyber breaches of dozens of congressmen, and more only had to do with Democrats.

The bank fraud charges are simple and straightforward. If anything, as attorneys who work on these types of cases told me, these charges are oddly simplistic. Typically, an affidavit seeking to make the case to indict someone in a bank fraud case, a case that is only the first step toward a much larger criminal investigation, would be much longer and more detailed. Perhaps one reason for the brevity of this affidavit—it's just over two thousand words, or the length of a magazine feature—is because it was written by an agent in his second year on the job. Still, there are many details reporters who read these documents are used to seeing that aren't there. When the FBI makes a case against a suspect, it generally includes a lot more background information and more details from the financial institutions impacted.

It's not like the Awans have simplistic holdings they could fit on the Internal Revenue Service's 1040EZ tax form. Complex real estate deals also connect the Awans. Hina Alvi bought two homes in Lorton, Virginia, in 2008, including one in which all the Awan brothers appear to have resided at one time or another. In November 2016, she sold that home to the youngest brother, Jamal, who was then only twenty-two years of age, for $620,000. The transaction capitalized on increasing Washington- area real estate appraisals, netting her $150,000. Imran, meanwhile, also owned a house in Springfield, Virginia, which he put in his father's name in 2008 for reasons we'll get into later, as they have to do with an entirely different set of issues related to Imran.

Agent Merriman does say that this "affidavit is submitted for the limited purpose of establishing probable cause. Because this affidavit is limited in purpose, it does not contain all information known to me, other law enforcement officers, or the United States Government."

That's an understatement. Its brevity is jarring to anyone used to seeing such reports.

Imran was arraigned the following day and pleaded not guilty to one count of bank fraud. He was ordered to surrender his passports, to abide by a curfew, and to wear a GPS device that would alert authorities if he strayed more than fifty miles from his primary residence in Virginia.

Representative Wasserman Schultz did finally fire Imran on July 25, after a lot of media began contacting her office to ask if she had any statement to make about her then arrested IT aide, a suspect she had long argued needed "due process" because she said he was only being investigated because he was a Muslim.

This is when Wasserman Schultz's office would say: "After details of the investigation were reviewed with us, my office was provided no evidence to indicate that laws had been broken, which over time, raised troubling concerns about due process, fair treatment, and potential ethnic and religious profiling. Upon learning of his arrest, he was terminated."

Weeks later, on August 17, 2017, a federal grand jury convened in the US District Court for the District of Columbia and indicted Awan and his wife on four counts, including conspiracy, making false statements, bank fraud, and unlawful monetary transactions.

The bank fraud case, laid out by Agent Merriman, is straightforward. Imran and Hina Alvi were charged with conspiring to obtain home equity loans for $165,000 and $120,000 from the Wright Patman Congressional Federal Credit Union in Oakton, Virginia, and transfer the money to Pakistan based on a series of lies to deceive the bank.

On January 18, 2017, the couple wired $283,000 from Hina Alvi's credit union checking account to two individuals in Faisalabad, Pakistan. This money, according to the charges filed, was obtained from the Wright Patman Congressional Federal Credit Union under false pretenses.

Still, the affidavit from the FBI didn't mention an investigation related to the procurement theft of congressional equipment or the many other facets of this case. Also, the other members of this IT team of House administrators had yet to be charged as this book was going to print.

On September 1, 2017, Imran Awan would plead not guilty to the charges. Though these charges might only be a footnote to what he has done and how he has impacted Democrats and perhaps the DNC, the bank fraud case is nevertheless very symbolic of his behavior.

Records from the Fairfax County Courthouse show that Hina Alvi purchased a home (4809 Sprayer Street, Alexandria, VA 22309) on November 7, 2014, for $187,500. Wright Patman Congressional Federal Credit Union is in the business of, among other things, loaning money to individuals who use a primary residence to secure such loans. One of those loans to Hina Alvi was for a "home equity line of credit." This can be used to pay off an original loan and/or take cash advances to a certain maximum.

Hina Alvi applied for the loan on or about December 12, 2016. As part of that loan application, she submitted her federal tax returns for 2014 and 2015. Those tax returns showed she filed jointly with her husband, Imran, and that they listed no rental income on their tax forms even though they were receiving income from renting proper-ties (more on this later, as one of Imran's tenants would turn over to investigators at least three BlackBerry smartphones and many laptops he found on the property). As part of her loan application, Hina Alvi also listed her W-2 income for 2015 as being $157,531.00, which matched the amount of income listed on her actual W-2 issued by the US House of Representatives. Also, on a portion of her loan applica-tion asking whether she had any other income, she didn't list any—again indicating she was not earning rental income.

To substantiate this, Agent Merriman interviewed an assistant vice president of security at the Wright Patman Congressional Federal Credit Union and found they don't normally provide home equity loans if the property isn't a primary residence, as rental properties are considered to be riskier types of collateral.

Then, on July 10, 2017, US Capitol Police special agent Sean A. Camp interviewed some of Imran and Hina Alvi's tenants who were living at the same property the Awans were trying to use to secure a home equity loan. These people rented the property from June/July 2015 through October 2016. One of the tenants said they found the property through a website that lists rental properties. Another tenant said the primary point of contact regarding the rental property was Imran.

A person who later rented a property from the Awans, Andre Taggart, says Imran said his name was "Alex" and that he was very evasive about his identity. This would happen after Imran knew he was under investigation.[2] At this time, Imran and his team were still employed with exorbitant salaries in Congress and were allegedly busy stealing House equipment.

Agent Merriman found these tenants were paying approximately two thousand dollars per month for rent and that their rent checks were written to "Suriaya Begiim or Begum." "Based upon information and belief, I know that Begum is Alvi's mother," said Agent Merriman.

Then, on July 24, 2017 (the day Imran was arrested), Special Agent Camp and Agent Merriman interviewed another tenant who'd rented the house Imran and Hina Alvi were calling their primary resi-dence on the loan application. This tenant lived with his family in the home from February 2016 through May 2017 and paid $2,100 per month to Hina Alvi.

Though the application for the loan also asked, "Do you intend to occupy the property as your primary residence?" Hina Alvi (or perhaps Imran acting as Hina Alvi) answered yes, even though she clearly wasn't living there. The application also asked for the "purpose of refinance," and Hina Alvi answered, "Cash out home improvement."

The bank asked for the sex of the person completing the form, and whoever completed the form answered "male." The application also asked for the phone number of the individual completing the form, and they gave the number (202) 604-7650. Agent Merriman found through records from Verizon that the person who held this number was in fact Imran. Also, a tenant of another rental property owned by Hina Alvi told Agent Merriman they communicated with Imran using the same phone number.

The loan application asked Hina Alvi to list all real estate she owned and whether it was being used for rental income. Imran did list the property in question on the form but again said that no rental income was being earned on that property. They also listed a property at 4387 Pembrook Village Dr., Alexandria, VA 22309 and stated that Hina Alvi earned $1,650 per month in rental income on that property.

With this false information, the bank moved on December 12, 2016, to approve the loan and sent Hina Alvi an invitation to electronically sign the loan application by emailing it to "imranawan1@ gmail.com." Agent Merriman had no trouble learning the obvious, that the email address "imranawan1@gmail.com" was Imran's. Agent Merriman said that "based on a review of the contents of this email account," he "does not believe that this email account was ever used by Alvi."

Next, records show that on that same day, "Alvi" (this was likely Imran) electronically signed the loan application. The computer internet protocol (IP) address used to sign and send the loan documents was 143.231.249.139. Agent Merriman says this "IP address belongs to the US House of Representatives, whose servers are located within the District of Columbia."

Then on January 3, 2017, a loan officer at the bank sent an email to "imranawan1@gmail.com" asking the following questions:

> Good Aftemoon [sic] Mr. Alvi,
>
> I received your file back from the Underwriter. There are a few items needed before a final approval can be received. I have listed below the pending documents needed:
>
> 1. Please provide a copy of the current lease agreement for rental 4387 Pembrook Village Dr., Alexandria, Virginia 22309...
>
> 4. Please write a statement why 2014 and 2015 tax returns are not showing rental income for 4387 Pembrook Village Dr., Alexandria VA...

On January 4, 2017, an email was sent from imranawan1@gmail.com to the loan officer stating:

> To Whom It May Concern:
>
> 4387 Pembrook Village Dr. Alexandria YA 22309 property was not on my 2014 and 2015 tax returns as a rental because it was not rent out during those years.
>
> Regards,
> Hina Alvi

On that same day, another email was also sent from imranawan1@gmail.com to the loan officer. Attached to that email was a residential lease agreement dated February 4, 2016, between Hina Alvi and her mother for the Pembrook Village property covering the dates March l, 2016, to March 1, 2018. Agent Merriman, however, soon found several other people who had rental agreements for that property during that same time.

Then, on January 5, 2017, an email from irnranawan1@gmail.com to the loan officer said:

Hi [Loan Officer]

When will you have an answer on both of our
HELOC approval? And what are the soonest closing dates please? Kindly advise…

The loan officer sent an email back stating that the loan was
approved for $165,000. The closing for the loan occurred on or about
January 12, 2017. As part of that closing, Hina Alvi was asked to exe-
cute an occupancy and financial status affidavit. On that affidavit, Hina
Alvi (again, likely Imran) stated that the property was used as her "principal residence" and that "Borrower will occupy and use the Property
as Borrower's principal residence within 60 days after Borrower signs
the Security Instrument. Borrower will continue to occupy and use the
property as Borrower's principal residence for at least one (1) year from
the date that Borrower first occupies the Property."

Of course, a tenant with a lease agreement was in the house at
this time.

"Based on our investigation," said Agent Merriman, "which
included physical surveillance and interviews of individuals, [I]
learned that [Imran] Awan and Alvi were residing at 9667 Hawkshead
Drive, Lorton, Virginia 22079 until on or about February 16, 2017.
On or after February 16, 2017, [they] resided at two other residences,
neither of which" was the property they were using to secure the loan.

Finally, on January 18, 2017, an international wire transfer
request form was submitted by Hina Alvi (or perhaps Imran) at the
Wright Patman Congressional Federal Credit Union branch at the
Longworth House Office Building in the amount of $283,000 to two
individuals in Faisalabad, Pakistan. On the international wire request
form, the contact number of (202) 225-0346 and an email address
of imranawan1@gmail.com were given. This raised a red flag, so on
January 18, 2017, a representative from the credit union called and
requested to speak to Hina Alvi.

"The person answering the call, who was a male, pretended that
he was Alvi," said Agent Merriman. "On the call, the representative
asked the man to verify the address of where the wire was being sent

and the purpose of the outgoing wire. The male speaking to the representative said that the purpose of the wire was 'funeral arrangements.' The [credit union] representative then stated that 'funeral arrangements' may not be an acceptable reason for the wire. The male speaking to the representative then responded that he would look online for an acceptable reason for the wire. After a long pause, the male said that the reason for the wire was 'buying property.' The representative accepted that reason and initiated the wire transfer to Pakistan. Bank records show that $165,000 of $283,000 wired to Pakistan was from the...loan for the Sprayer Street Property."

For these basic reasons, Agent Merriman says Imran and Hina Alvi "engaged in a scheme to defraud [the credit union] by obtaining a... loan based on two material misrepresentations."

That would seem to be a very clear case of bank fraud, but it's also like charging Al Capone only with tax evasion, as if a mobster whose crew was gunning people down on the streets of Chicago as they ran alcohol during Prohibition was only guilty of not paying taxes on the illegal spirits. Certainly, authorities should use all tools available to convict a known criminal, but it isn't as if getting witnesses to speak in this case would be as difficult as it was in the tommy-gun days of Al Capone.

The chief of staff in Rep. Yvette Clarke's office who agreed to sign away $120,000 in missing computer equipment for Imran in early 2016, for example, likely would have struck a deal in a heartbeat to stay out of court and save her career. Also, a previous tenant of Imran's, Andre Taggart, found BlackBerries and laptop computers in the garage of the home he was renting from the Awans and turned them over to the authorities. Taggart says the computer equipment had "government markings" on it that he recognized, as he had dealt with government computer equipment when he was a US Marine (he was in the service for fourteen years). Taggart has been very open about his eagerness to help prosecutors however he can (more on this incredible part of the tale in chapter 5), but he says the authorities have only asked him a few questions.

Ultimately, after Imran was arrested on July 24, 2017, mainstream news outlets were forced to address the criminal investigation and related scandal and cover-up. Though they had to mention it, many in the media would do all they could to downplay the story.

The New York Times would run a "news article" a few days after Imran's arrest that sounded like a smarmy *Times* Broadway critic pooh-poohing a play that dared to step out of the *Times'* politically correct worldview:

> For months, conservative news outlets have built a case against Imran Awan, his wife, two brothers and a friend, piece by piece.
>
> To hear some commentators tell it, with the help of his family and a cushy job on Capitol Hill, Mr. Awan, a Pakistani-American, had managed to steal computer hardware, congressional data and even—just maybe—a trove of internal Democratic National Committee emails that eventually surfaced last summer on WikiLeaks. It helped that the story seems to involve, if only tangentially, Debbie Wasserman Schultz, the Florida congresswoman who is the former chairwoman of the committee and an ally of Hillary Clinton's.
>
> The Daily Caller, with almost two dozen articles on the family, has led the pack in reporting the story, packaging new details that have dribbled out of the investigation into a growing web of material, even as few in the mainstream news media paid attention.
>
> That is until Monday, when Mr. Awan was arrested by the F.B.I. and United States Capitol Police on seemingly unrelated charges as he tried to board a flight to Pakistan. In the days since, the story has raced down an increasingly familiar track at warp speed, from the fringes of the internet to Fox News and other established publications.
>
> By Thursday morning, President Trump gave an added boost to the intrigue, reposting a tweet

from the conservative news site Townhall suggesting a cover-up by TV networks.

"ABC, NBC, and CBS Pretty Much Bury IT Scandal Engulfing Debbie Wasserman Schultz's Office," Townhall wrote, adding a link to an article explaining Mr. Awan's ties to the Florida Democrat.

But for all the publicity, few if any of the fundamental facts of the case have come into focus....[3]

And *The New York Times* would show no interest in bringing the facts into focus. It's "all the news that's fit to print" filter just wouldn't stand for this scandal and criminal investigation that has so much to do with Democrats in Congress.

There is no shortage of questions mainstream media publications would ask if all of this had to do solely with Republicans. Why did Rep. Debbie Wasserman Schultz keep Imran on the payroll even after he was banned from accessing Congress's network? Why did she keep paying his wife until after she took her kids to Pakistan? Even though Imran couldn't work on the House network after February 2, 2017, people reported still seeing him in congressional buildings. Why? Did he blackmail Wasserman Schultz? After all, he had access to her private emails and to what she did when she ran the Democratic National Committee. Do the Awans know something about the DNC's power play to rig the game in Hillary Clinton's favor? What about the missing computer equipment? Why was Imran copying terabytes of congressmen's data to a server he controlled? Why did he and his brothers access this server thousands of times even though they weren't authorized to do so? Was the data they retrieved sold to a foreign country or other group?

Several attorneys who work on legal actions related to Congress, but who wanted their names kept out of print, pointed out that some in Congress would like to avoid having congressional Democrats and their staff members deposed in a criminal investigation, as depositions can come out via Freedom of Information Act requests. Judicial Watch, which has had a lot of success with FOIA requests and via lawsuits filed in federal court, has been very involved in demanding answers in this case.

Just imagine what Representative Wasserman Schultz might say if she were deposed. Or how about the person who succeeding her at the DNC, Donna Brazile, who wrote a tell-all book about her time at the DNC. Brazile might, *gasp*, tell the truth. How about other IT aides who work in Congress and who have given a lot of insight for this book? What might they say? How about the congressional staffers who heard Imran say what he could have done to people in Pakistan?

Or how about Hina Alvi? As we'll see in the next chapter, she returned to the United States, likely with a plea deal. And she is a woman scorned, as she accused Imran of illegally marrying another woman in a secret ceremony in Pakistan.

That and other bombshells that could intrigue both federal prosecutors and Jerry Springer's audience were about to come out.

CHAPTER 4

WITNESS FOR THE PROSECUTION

For the sake of money, they would have done anything.

—One of Imran Awan's relatives[1]

The courtroom was as quiet as a chapel before mass as Imran Awan sat nervously in a hardwood chair checking his black digital watch every half minute. He was slouched over a long wooden table at the front of the courtroom. He might have looked dapper in his smart blue suit and white shirt with the top button undone if he didn't look so troubled. A white-and-blue-striped tie hung loosely over his knees that waved at the floor as he sat up and leaned over the table again and again like a man working oars. Between glances at his watch, he'd toss his head furtively toward the door of the courtroom.

The few journalists in the courtroom knew what was bothering Imran. His wife—at least his first one—had come back from Pakistan and was due to be arraigned the same day. None of us knew if he'd seen her since she'd returned a few days before, as Imran and Hina Alvi were living in different residences. The reason why, we all supposed, was that police reports had gone public showing that Imran had relations with two other women in Virginia.

The journalists in attendance were seated on benches lined up like church pews facing the front of courtroom number two at the US District Court for the District of Columbia. It was a Friday morning in early October 2017, and it was bright and warm outside, but there were no windows in the courtroom affording a view to those inside.

People's feet were shuffling on the hard floor, and conversations were politely muffled. Anyone who knew the background could surely feel the drama in the sparsely filled courtroom, as Imran's wife, Hina Alvi Awan, had likely returned from Pakistan with a deal from the US Department of Justice. She was officially scheduled as a "walk in" and was to be arraigned at this same hearing.

Hina Alvi had left for Pakistan with their three children about two months after the investigation by Capitol Police became known. While she was gone, on August 17, 2017, a federal grand jury indicted Awan and her on four counts, including conspiracy and conspiring to obtain home equity loans for $165,000 and $120,000 from the Wright Patman Congressional Federal Credit Union and transferring the money to Pakistan.

Those charges are politically trumped-up nonsense, according to Imran's attorney, Chris Gowen, who is a founding partner of Gowen Rhoades Winograd & Silva. He sat in a chair to Imran's left and leaned close to chat with him. Gowen's red hair is thin and fading. He wears a patchy beard and dark-rimmed glasses and has the rumpled look of a man used to wearing business suits, which look to be purposely too large to accommodate his middle-aged weight settling low in his gut. His eyes are quick, and he has an accomplished political background that has taught him not to admit anything, just to attack—perhaps a lesson learned from president Bill Clinton's "War Room," as Gowen worked for the Clinton administration and was so trusted he even helped out as a fact-checker for President Clinton's memoir, *My Life*. He also directed advance operations for Hillary Clinton's 2008 presidential campaign. But he doesn't put all that at the top of his résumé; instead, he boasts he was the only attorney in Pennsylvania to "have a prenuptial agreement set aside for breach of contract when both parties were still alive."

As Gowen whispered to Imran, they were actually facing the prosecutor's table—the defense and prosecutor's tables didn't face the judge's bench, as they do in so many courtrooms, but faced each other.

Just then, assistant US attorney Michael Marando and two others in dark suits came to the table across from them, plunked down their attaché cases, opened them, and pulled papers out.

Imran and Gowen would have to look to their right to see Judge Tanya S. Chutkan, a judge appointed by president Barack Obama in 2013. Chutkan was born in Jamaica and earned her law degree in 1987 from the University of Pennsylvania Law School. She was a trial attorney and supervisor at the Public Defender Service for the District of Columbia from 1991 to 2002. She then went back into private practice before being nominated for the federal court. Her husband, Peter Arno Krauthamer, is also a judge. He was a public defender in DC and later taught at Howard University. He is on the bench at the Superior Court of the District of Columbia and was also nominated by President Obama. He got his appointment in 2011.

So the presiding judge in this hyper-political case having much to do with Democrats was nominated by a Democrat, and Imran's attorney had worked for both Bill and Hillary Clinton. Though justice is ideally blind, any lawyer will tell you, if only during off-the-record conversations, that the politics of the judge all too often matters a great deal. But then, this is the US District Court for the District of Columbia, not the US District Court for the Northern District of Alabama, where a judge's politics are apt to be quite different.

Surely everyone involved in this case is aware that the preferred politics of much of the Washington media and of many officials in the District were offering public cover for this cancer of a case. The hearing was scheduled on a Friday, and the next would be scheduled for a Tuesday just two days before Thanksgiving—the judge and both attorneys actually laughed when they agreed on that date.

The journalists in the room could be counted with a glance. Luke Rosiak, a reporter with the *Daily Caller* who has been all over this case, was there. There was a young blogger who drove in from Ocean City, Maryland, who told me he came to "cover his first big case."

And then there was George Webb, a self-described citizen journalist whom *The New York Times* panned as "a prolific right-wing YouTube conspiracy theorist"[2] but who is actually a Democrat who says he proudly voted for Barack Obama twice and gave money to Bernie Sanders's campaign for president.[3] He says the *Times* didn't talk to him and clearly didn't watch his stuff before labeling him as "right wing." He even said he'd contacted the reporter, but Nicholas Fandos didn't respond to him—the narrative had been set, and Webb only fit if he was right wing.

Webb, though, does give a good impression of a YouTube conspiracy theorist. He spent much of his career as a salesperson but has increasingly been drawn into chasing stories no one else will cover. He has the air of Mel Gibson's character Jerry Fletcher in the 1997 movie *Conspiracy Theory*. He is very smart and speaks fast and has filed, as this was being written, three lawsuits against federal officials. He names himself as the plaintiff and his defendants include Andrew McCabe, former deputy director of the FBI, and Peter Strzok, former director of counterintelligence for the FBI. (Strzok was moved from this post and back-benched to the FBI's human resources department after it was found he was sending texts to his girlfriend that were very anti-president Donald J. Trump at a time when Strzok was helping to investigate possible collusion between Russia and the Trump administration.)

I admit it isn't all that kind to compare Webb to Gibson's character, who was a New York City cab driver so obsessed by every crackpot theory passed along as "suppressed news" on talk radio or the internet that he published and mailed out a newsletter on his theories to his audience of seven people. But nevertheless, it is an apt comparison. Webb's YouTube videos are often close-ups of his face as he speaks fast and low, almost like he is whispering excitedly in an underground bunker. After he told me he'd been illegally jailed for pursuing a corruption story, I asked more questions and he said local authorities had found him sleeping in his car and thought him suspicious enough to take in for questioning. He says this happened because a higher-up from Washington contacted the local police and told them to be on the lookout for him. After speaking to Webb, I thought there could have been another reason.

Still, like Gibson's character, Webb just might be right about this one. Even though his court filings often make giant leaps to connect dots, Webb is poking the system in its soft spots and getting some telling reactions.

It should also be said that Webb wouldn't be left to wander so much with this story if just a few Washington journalists had taken a day off from the Trump-Russia collusion investigation to point a curious and cynical eye at this case.

So those were the characters in the thinly populated courtroom scene in this multifaceted international crime drama.

All heads turned when Hina Alvi Awan entered the courtroom with her attorney, Nikki Lotze, from the firm Lotze Mosley LLP.

Hina Alvi is short and heavy and was in a dark business suit, with her black hair professionally pulled back. She sat across from Imran, facing him and with her back to the prosecutor's table, but her eyes never went to Imran's. Though Imran tried to make eye contact with her frequently through the entire court appearance, he would only succeed fleetingly. His body language was inviting and he began to smile; he looked all of a sudden like a charming man just trying and trying to find an in.

As for Hina Alvi, whether she had a plea deal or not, infidelity issues were likely part of the reason for her newfound ability to ignore his charming advances. At this time, few knew she had already filed charges in Pakistan against Imran for illegally, and secretly, marrying another woman.

Police reports in Virginia, however, had already come out showing that two different women had called the police seeking protection from Imran. One of these women, Sumaira Siddique, is the one he allegedly wed in Pakistan even though he was still then legally married to Hina Alvi.

Hina Alvi filed papers against Imran in Pakistan on September 13, 2017, for polygamy. Her complaint said in part:

Respondent has contract a second marriage on 17-08-2015 with one Mst. Sumaira Shehzadi alias Sumaira Siddique...without obtaining prior permission. Rather he mentioned himself as bachelor in...marriage certificate, he falsely declared that he has no wife or biological children at the time of contracting second marriage. This act of the respondent was shocking for the complainant and she asked the respondent about his second marriage on which he became furious while admitting the same and said he has no need to obtain permission from the complainant....

He further said furiously that the complainant has no right or power to restrain him from second and even third marriage. Furthermore, the respondent threatened the complainant of dire consequences, he also threatened to harm the lives of family of the complainant if she intervenes into the affairs of the respondent.

Sumaira Siddique, the alleged second wife named in Hina Alvi's Pakistani legal petition, had actually called Virginia police on July 28, 2016, to say she felt Imran was keeping her "like a slave" in a Virginia apartment and to ask how she might apply for a protection order.

The Calls for Service Report filed by the police officer said, "Siddique called in regards to a man that she claims is her boyfriend. The man she is referring to is married to another woman. Siddique and this other man do not live together nor do they have any children in common. Ms. Siddique lives in one of the other man's apartments. Ms. Siddique informed me that she feels like a slave to this man because he is married to this other woman. Ms. Siddique feels that this man is bringing her down and wants him out of her life. Ms. Siddique wanted info on how to obtain a restraining order against him."[4]

Just after Hina Alvi filed her complaint, a few journalists in Pakistan looked into her story. On September 29, 2016, Abid Khan, a reporter with ARY News, wrote: "Hina Alvi, through her counsel advocate Hafiz Ahsan-ul-Haq, filed an application in a local court that she married Imran Awan in 2005 and both lived in the United States. However, during her recent visit to Pakistan, she learnt that Awan has remarried secretly, fraudulently and without her consent with another woman named Sumaira Siddique. Alvi said that she was completely unaware that her husband has remarried illegally and without justification and was not even registered in the union council. Therefore, she pleaded that Awan should be tried under marriage laws for contracting the second marriage without her permission."[5]

It appears that Imran also had a mistress on the side. The third woman we know about also called Virginia police to seek protection from Imran. Her name is Salam Chaudry, and she is also originally from Pakistan. A December 27, 2016, police Incident/Investigation Report said:

> On December 27th I responded to the Manitoba Apartment complex for a Domestic Dispute. When I arrived I met with Chaudhry Salam. Ms. Salam told me that she believed her roomate, Imran Awan, was not supposed to live there and she wanted him to leave. I spoke to Mr. Awan who advised that he was on the lease and later it was determined by Ms Salam that he was. I explained the eviction process to Ms. Salam and she said "Ive heard that before". It was difficult at first to determine what was really going on as both parties were not cooperating fully with the investigation. I had Ms. Salam step into the back portion of the house away from her "roomate". I asked her what the relation was between the two. She said they are just friends and told me she had come here from Pakistan. It appeared that the two

people were in a romantic relationship. Ms Salam had a [redacted] that she said happened when she was doing dishes. Ms. Salam said she just wanted to leave and go to a shelter as she has no money. Ms. Salam has two children that were both at the residence both under the age of 8. I asked Ms. Salam why she was crying and calling the police. Ms. Salam insisted nothing happened but that she wanted to leave. I went and spoke to Mr. Awan who quickly advised that he wanted to speak with a lawyer. I asked him about the small amount of dried blood that appeared to be on his left hand. He stated that it was from when his "roomate" was getting the phone from him. Ms. Salam also insisted that it was an incidental blood transfer from her hand to his whe[n] he was handed her a phone. Ms. Salam began packing up the children and was getting ready to leave. I spoke to Mr. Awan and asked if he would mind finding a hotel for the night or possibly staying with friends or family. He said he is "not welcome" to stay with his family but after some convincing he said he would leave the apartment for the night. After he left I stayed and spoke with Ms. Salam about getting a protective order. It appeared as if the two are in some type of committed relationship but both parties denied this. Ms Salam and her two children stayed in the apartment and I advised her to call if anything else happened.[6]

If Imran was supporting, to some extent, three women with five children between them, then he certainly had an expensive romantic life to pay for. To do so effectively, he would have also needed to be secretive about his money so that each of the three women wouldn't become aware he was supporting the other two. Of course, Hina

Alvi, at this time, did have an annual salary of about $160,000 from Congress, and she did own some properties, though tenants at some of these properties have said they dealt with Imran, not Hina Alvi, so it's unclear who was getting the rent money.

Though it is difficult to say just how the money flowed between the Awans, the possible second wife, and the mistress, it is alleged that Imran also took part in a fraud to obtain funds from his father. We know this because another woman, Imran's stepmother, also called Virginia police and filed a legal complaint.

In a civil case, Imran's stepmother, Samina Gilani, said Abid Awan, who was also on the House of Representatives payroll thanks to Imran, tried to steal a $50,000 life insurance policy from her. She even accused Imran of keeping her from her husband while he was on his deathbed and said that Imran had placed devices in her home to record her conversations.

A police report in Virginia on January 5, 2017, said:

> Samani Galani called DPSC after her step children were denying her access to her husband of 8 years, Muhammad Shah, who is currently hospitalized. Upon arrival Samina indicated she did not speak English and an Urdu translator with Language Line was used. Samina stated her husband has been in the hospital for several months and she has visited him several times. She stated she was denied access at her last visit. I made contact with her stepson, Abid, who responded to location and was obviously upset with the situation. He stated he has full power of attorney over his father and produced an unsigned, undated, document as proof. He stated his father is undergoing cancer treatment and Samina is causing more stress upon him and the family. He refused to disclose his father's location. I was further advised that her husband did not want contact with her at this

time but was scheduled to return to the house within a week.[7]

Imran's father, Muhammad Shah (he also went by the surname Ashraf), would die of cancer on January 16, 2017. Gilani says Shah was injured in a car accident in 2007 in Pakistan, a wreck that killed his first wife. He got insurance money and government disability payments in the United States as a result, but "Imran Awan took Mr. Ashraf's money fraudulently by signing legal documents with phony/fake signatures" at that time, too, she said. Sometime after 2007, Shah married Gilani. She doesn't speak English and has needed interpreters to deal with the authorities.

All of this has come out because Gilani filed a complaint with a Virginia court stating that some of Shah's sons had tried to steal a $50,000 life insurance policy Shah had taken out with Americo in 2012, a policy naming Gilani as the primary beneficiary. But on November 16, 2016, as Shah lay on his deathbed, Americo received an Ownership Change Request form that would put Abid in charge of administrative decisions in regard to the policy. Then, on January 11, five days before Shah would die, Abid tried to use this newly gained power to make himself the beneficiary of the policy instead of Gilani. The form required a witness's signature, but that box was left blank, so the change request was rejected. A week later, Abid resubmitted the form with a notary's seal.

After Shah died, Americo received a claim on February 2 asking that the $50,000 be paid to Abid. But Americo told the court it also received a letter from Gilani contending the "beneficiary changes to the policy were procured through fraud."

Abid countered this by saying he'd "recorded by videotape the signing of the ownership change" in anticipation of problems. Abid sent the video to Americo. But a signature line asking for the spouse of the previous owner to consent was left blank on the form Shah signed; also, a line asking for the signature of a witness was signed by Abid's wife.

Due to these competing claims, Americo said it couldn't "safely determine who is rightfully entitled to the policy proceeds" and asked the court to resolve the issue.

In April 2018, a Virginia court ruled in favor of Abid, granting him $45,000 of the $50,000 life insurance payout ($5,000 went to the insurance company for expenses related to the dispute). Gilani had previously declined to split the money with Abid. "I didn't do the deal because they had been adopting bad behaviors. I cannot agree to that. It wasn't about the money," Gilani said through an interpreter.

Abid hired James Bacon, a high-profile attorney with Allred, Bacon, Halfhill & Young PC. Gilani hired the best she could afford, Michael Hadeed, a business attorney who was convicted in 2010 of conspiracy and immigration fraud and, as a result, had his license to practice law taken away for two years.[8]

During the hearing, Hadeed failed to offer any evidence to the judge that could have shown a possible pattern of fraud by Abid—a pattern that has been written about in the media. Hadeed didn't even question the mental capacity of Shah as he lay on his deathbed. Hadeed also withdrew allegations of fraud and agreed that the case should be decided solely on the insurance contract's language.

After the court hearing, Hadeed told reporters Bacon had threatened to sue him for defamation. "I don't want to get myself in a lawsuit over this," he said.

Months before this hearing, Gilani also said that Imran had demanded she sign a Pakistani power of attorney enabling the brothers to take possession of property owned by their father there. "I was put under tremendous pressure to sign the power of attorney to Mr. Shahid Imran Awan for Pakistani properties," said Gilani.

In a court filing, Samina Gilani explains the situation this way:

> During his Visit to Pakistan Mr Ashraf got sick in Pakistan and got admitted in a hospital in October. Due to his severe health conditions he was brought back to USA and was taken to the local hospital the same day of our arrival....During

his illness (while Mr Ashraf was in hospital) his children barred me from seeing Mr Ashraf many times. Last time I was taken to Mr Ashraf was 12-31-2016. Between 12-31-2016 and 01-16-2017 was completely denied by Mr Ashrafs children to visit him in hospital. Meanwhile all relevant papers and 2 lap top computers were also taken from my house illegally without my permission and knowledge.

Now some more details about the behaviour of Mr Ashraf's children, during Mr Ashraf's illness while he was admitted in hospital my telephone conversations were taped and some other recording devices were also installed/planted in my house at 6314 Thomas Drive, Springfield, VA. I was directed by Mr Ashraf's children not to go out or visit Mr Ashraf without the children's permission, only the children will decide when to see Mr Ashraf.

Some times between 12-31-2016 and 01-16-2017 (believed to be on January 6, 2017) I called the local police to find out the where abouts of my husband Mr Ashraf since I was completely blacked out about my husband. I had no Knowledge of my husband nor of his health conditions. I did inform this situation to the police over the phone and in person when the police arrived at my house. At that time one of Mr Ashraf's son Abid Awan showed up and spoke to the police and painted a picture of family matter to the police.

Right after the police left Mr Ashraf's another son Shahid Imran Awan showed up and threatened me for me calling the police. Mr Shahid Imran Awan threatened that he is very powerful and if I ever call the police again Mr Shehid

Imran Awan will do harm to me and my family members back in Pakistan and one of my cousins here in Baltimore. Mr Shahid Imran Awan threatened that he has power to kidnap my family members back in Pakistan. Mr Shahid Imran Awan did admit to me that my phone is taped and there are devices installed in the house to listen my all conversations and that he will remove all these devices. Next day of the police calling Mr Shahid Imran Awan came back to my house at 6314 Thomas drive and removed something from under the kitchen counter and living room from behind the printer), after he left I checked under kitchen counter and found some marks and took pictures of that place pictures are sent to you. Worth mentioning here that Shahid Imran Awan introduces himself someone from US congress or someone from Federal Agencies. Mr Shahid Imran Awan also demanded me to sign a power of Attorney for my Pakistani matters and was forcing me over the phone and through other people to sign power of attorney. I was put under tremendous pressure to sign the power of attorney to Mr Shahid Imran Awan for Pakistani properties and at point I was going to sign, but then I decided to leave my house and requested my sisters to arrange my departure from that location....

In Pakistan Mr Shahid Imran Awan manages to have police mobile based on his position in US congress or Federal Agencies to escort him during his visit to Pakistan. There are many people who have this knowledge that my phone conversations were taped and my conversations in side my house were being listened.

All that might just be a family squabble over money worthy of a local court, if not a Bravo TV series, if the Awans didn't also have so much to do with members of Congress. By letting this family gain access to their offices, their emails, and other personal information, as well as their budgets and official expenditures, the forty or more Democrats who employed the Awans and their associates not only opened themselves and their offices to possible theft, but also allowed a criminal probe to open a window into everything they said and did. This is undoubtedly part of the reason why Democrats in Congress have been loath to address the Awan situation.

With all of that rumbling thunderously in the background, Hina Alvi's attorney, Nikki Lotze, sat beside her and leaned over the table to chat with Chris Gowen. Lotze graduated from Georgetown Law in 1993. She has blonde hair parted on the side that just goes to her ears and a face that looks surprisingly like the Queen of Hearts in Disney's 1951 animated version of *Alice in Wonderland*. Minutes before, just outside the courtroom, she repeated the refrain that there was nothing to see here by saying she didn't know what Imran's relationships with other women had to do with the case. As an experienced attorney, she must know such legal and public disputes offer real opportunities for federal prosecutors to turn her client against Imran Awan and even to extract a confession from Hina Alvi.

It seemed likely that Hina Alvi did get a deal from the Justice Department. Weeks before, US attorneys had asked the court to quash an outstanding arrest warrant for her so she wouldn't be put in handcuffs when she arrived back in the United States with her children. Such a request certainly gives the impression that a deal was negotiated by her attorney. Clearly this means, if her attorney knew what she is doing, that the deal was good enough to convince Hina Alvi to come back to the United States to face an arraignment on the bank fraud charges and possibly much more.

Documents filed in federal court in September 2017 said, "Counsel represented that defendant Alvi will turn in her passport(s) when she returns to the United States, and that she will not seek to book any international travel following her appearance in the United

States."[9] At the hearing, she would turn over her US passport. When asked if she also had a passport from Pakistan, she said yes but that she would have to find it before she could turn it over. She was then arraigned and pleaded not guilty.

By this time, Imran had already pleaded not guilty to the bank fraud charges. That was after a grand jury returned an indictment in the US District Court for the District of Columbia charging the couple with a total of four counts.

During a previous status hearing, Imran had requested that a GPS monitoring anklet be taken off. By the time of this hearing, in October 2017, the tracking device had been attached to Imran since his arrest the previous July. That fight over whether Imran should be monitored electronically would continue. Just before Christmas 2017, US attorney Jessie Liu, a Harvard- and Yale-educated attorney from Texas who was nominated by president Donald J. Trump in June 2017 to head the US Attorney's Office for the District of Columbia, filed a motion calling Imran a "flight risk" who might very well flee to Pakistan if let out of the High Intensity Supervision Program requiring him to follow an electronically monitored midnight-to-6:00-a.m. curfew and limit travel to a 150-mile radius of his residence.

"While the government possesses Awan's Pakistani passport, nothing prevents him from obtaining a new Pakistani passport at the Embassy in D.C. That passport would permit Awan to board a flight and leave the country at any time," said the court motion. US attorney Liu noted that Imran has "strong ties" to property in Pakistan and said that, because he transferred tens of thousands of dollars there, he could "clearly maintain a life in that country."

Liu was referring to a controversial land deal in which Imran is involved back in Pakistan. To obtain loans from the Wright Patman Congressional Federal Credit Union, Imran told the bank he needed to transfer the money to buy property in Pakistan. The particulars of that land deal are complex and have been locally controversial in Pakistan, but Imran's attorney, Chris Gowen, clearly has been aware of this property. After acknowledging to the *Daily Caller* that Imran sent money to a member of the Faisalabad police department, Gowen said the money was paid to the police officer "to make payments" on land. "You need to understand how land purchases work in Pakistan, and I don't have time to explain it to you," said Gowen.[10]

This land deal was also mentioned by Samina Gilani. Gilani said in a court statement that after Muhammad Shah's wife was killed in a car accident, he was supposed to get some "compensation" from "insurance" and "government benefits." According the *Daily Caller*, Gilani says her husband told her, "Imran Awan took Mr. Ashraf's all money fraudulently by signing legal documents with Phony/Fake signatures, Pretending to be Mr. Ashraf" in Pakistan. She says both Imran and Abid Awan were involved in this fraud. She also said, "After taking his money Shahid Imran Awan purchased real estate properties with that money."

Wajid Syed, a Washington correspondent for Pakistani television network Geo, followed this lead and found that the Awan brothers likely used their father's money to invest in two "housing colonies" in Faisalabad, Pakistan, called Gulshan e-Moeen and Gulshan e-Farid.

Nevertheless, Imran's attorney and former Bill and Hillary Clinton employee Gowen would say the US attorney's opposition to allowing Imran to take off his monitoring device was "solely for political purposes."

Liu, however, said in the motion: "Alvi departed abruptly with her two children to Pakistan.... Alvi only returned to the United States after the government arrested her husband, thereby preventing him from joining his wife and children in Pakistan."

Clearly Imran, who has money and ties to property in Pakistan, and who still maintains a dual citizenship with Pakistan, would be a flight risk until the legal actions against him run their course, but Judge Tanya Chutkan would say in court that she would see removing the restrictions more favorably as the weeks went by.

Chutkan is the same federal judge who, in December 2017, ordered the Health and Human Services Department to take two seventeen-year-old girls who'd been caught crossing the border from Mexico into the United States to an abortion facility. Judge Chutkan also ordered government officials not to tell anyone else about the abortions—not even their parents. Chutkan said she was acting to preserve the girls' "constitutional right to decide whether to carry their pregnancies to term"[11] even though they are not American citizens.

The two dual citizens of the United States and Pakistan in this case, Imran and Hina Alvi, stood when Judge Chutkan entered the courtroom and it was called to order.

Heading the prosecution's table, across from Imran and Hina Alvi, was assistant US attorney Michael Marando. He earned his undergraduate and law degrees from Cornell. In 2015 he married JoAnna Wasserman. The ceremony was officiated by Rainey R. Brandt, a District of Columbia Superior Court magistrate judge.[12] JoAnna Wasserman opted to keep her maiden name. Wasserman is the manager of education initiatives at the US Holocaust Memorial Museum in Washington. Her parents are Donna and Mark L. Wasserman of Baltimore, Maryland.

A spokesperson for Marando declined to say whether JoAnna Wasserman is related to Rep. Debbie Wasserman Schultz, who was born in Queens, New York, but a search at Ancestry.com didn't find a branch in their family trees in common. Internet rumors, nonetheless, made this claim. More interesting is that Debbie Wasserman Schultz's brother, Steven Wasserman, is also an assistant district attorney in the US Attorney's Office for the District of Columbia. Internet rumors did fly claiming that Steven Wasserman was to litigate the case against Imran and Hina Alvi, Representative Wasserman Schultz's former IT aides. Of course, that rumor didn't turn out to be true, but nevertheless there is an odd number of Wassermans in this mix.

Steven Wasserman did step into the politics of this case by tweeting: "The uproar over Rep. Debbie Wasserman Schultz and a now-fired information technology employee who faces a bank fraud charge appears to be much ado about not much."[13] Though it is hard to blame someone for defending their sister, perhaps one would think etiquette and better judgment would have restrained Steven Wasserman from commenting publicly, as he is an assistant US attorney in the very office prosecuting Representative Wasserman Schultz's former IT aides.

Amid all that background noise, Gowen again argued that Imran should be able to take the ankle tracking device off. Gowen cited the fact that Imran's wife, Hina Alvi, and their children were now in America and she wasn't wearing a tracking device; therefore, he should be able to lose his.

Even Judge Chutkan smirked when Gowen made this claim. Marando objected and noted that Imran often traveled to Pakistan for long stays without Hina Alvi or the kids. If Marando knew of the allegations about a second wife, he didn't say so, but by then the police reports showing that Imran allegedly kept two mistresses, one being the woman he allegedly married in a secret ceremony in Pakistan, had already gone public. Also, if Hina Alvi was to move about without a tracking device as part of a plea deal, Marando wasn't thus far making that public.

Instead, Marando argued that Imran's continued deception, his real estate interests in Pakistan, and the $283,000 he'd wired there in January 2017 all made it clear he was a flight risk. Everyone could also plainly see that the couple, Imran and Hina Alvi, had entered the courtroom separately and that they had different lawyers. Also, Gowen told Judge Chutkan that Imran and Hina Alvi were staying in separate residences. This, and the alleged polygamy charge against Imran, should lead any reasonable person to conclude that Hina Alvi didn't offer a big enough incentive for Imran to stay and face these charges in the United States, if indeed he could escape back to Pakistan.

As a specific example of Imran's deception, Marando said, "Two phones were found on [Imran] when he was arrested at Dulles International. One of the phones had been wiped clean just a few hours before."

This is when Gowen jumped in to say, "Awan had recently bought the phone, so of course it didn't have any data on it."

Marando then said the FBI found that the phone had been wiped on purpose. As previously noted, a time stamp on the iPhone indicated it had been wiped at 6:30 p.m. that evening. Marando postulated that Imran likely knew he'd be stopped and interrogated at the airport, as his wife had been stopped and searched there, so he wiped the phone.

When Marando pointed out that the defendants are from Pakistan, Judge Chutkan quickly dismissed that as immaterial. Marando backed this up by citing Imran's many trips to Pakistan. He might have also brought up payments Imran allegedly made to a police officer in Pakistan, a cousin of his, and a shady real estate deal in Pakistan Imran has been involved in. But he didn't take the argument into those complex issues; instead, he noted that a résumé had been found on Imran when he was arrested at Dulles International Airport listing a made-up address in Queens, New York. Marando speculated that perhaps Awan intended to move to New York City under this alias.

Judge Chutkan soon agreed to keep the monitor on Imran but said she'd be much more willing to hear arguments that it was no longer necessary in the coming weeks.

In another twist, Gowen brought up the computer found in April 2017 in the Rayburn House Office Building that Rep. Debbie Wasserman Schultz wanted back so badly she actually threatened the chief of the Capitol Police in a public hearing with "consequences" if it was not returned. Gowen argued that the computer and documents seized in the bag were "protected by attorney-client privilege." Gowen told the judge he planned to file a motion to get them returned by Capitol Police. In other words, he hopes to use this motion to quash the evidence.

The fight over this computer, and all it holds, would delay the next status hearing for Imran and Hina Alvi, as Judge Chutkan agreed to give more time to the defense to prepare a legal argument designed to get this laptop and whatever secrets it holds away from the authorities. In late November 2017, Chutkan ruled: "Additional time is necessary for the Defendants to review and analyze legal issues in this case and to review additional discovery provided by the government since the last status conference in this matter, and to review the voluminous discovery already produced by the government to the Defendants."

Part of that "voluminous discovery" is actually a copy of the contents of the laptop Imran allegedly left in the Rayburn building. If you're wondering what this laptop, and whatever is on it, is doing in a bank fraud case, then you've hit on one of the many clues showing this case is about a lot more than bank fraud.

The hard-drive copy was included in discovery even though Representative Wasserman Schultz has said the laptop contains House information and is a government-paid worker's computer, even though Imran was fired and banned from the House network because of suspected cybersecurity violations. None of that seems to have anything to do with bank fraud charges related to lying on forms to send almost $300,000 to Pakistan.

Marando, however, seemed embarrassed. He said this data was actually mistakenly given to Gowen under discovery and the Department of Justice wanted it back. This leads any interested observer to wonder if some low-level person at the DOJ simply provided the defense with all the materials in the ongoing DOJ file (which would include evidence the department might use from the FBI and Capitol Police to press other charges) and not just the evidence having to do with bank fraud charges.

This little squabble also made Judge Chutkan smirk, which showed once again that one of the great protectors of an open democratic government remains the size and incompetence of the government, as facts have many ways of escaping the large, bureaucratic, often ego-centric, partisan, and cumbersome system.

Then, in an argument designed to show hardship for then-jobless Imran Awan, Gowen said Imran had tried to become an Uber driver to earn money but that right-wing zealots had driven him out of that job. He said that as a result of this hatred and anti-Muslim bigotry, Imran was out of work and living in a "one-bedroom apartment." When Marando disputed this economic hardship argument, Gowen said he'd show the court Imran's Uber credentials. Marando tossed his head at this, but indeed Gowen later said outside the courtroom that Imran has been suspended by Uber due to "right-wing media attention."

Though such squabbles feel like drama for an episode of a television court series, not a case involving massive theft of congressional computer equipment and huge data breaches of congressmen's emails, it is such details that make people take plea deals and even speak to the media to give their side of the sordid story.

Meanwhile, other witnesses exposed more of the evolving tale and all it has to do with the sanctity of American freedom.

CHAPTER 5

THE POLITICAL CORRECTNESS FACTOR

You don't stop being a Marine 'cause you get out.

—Andre Taggart, a former tenant
of Imran Awan, after alerting authorities
to laptops and smartphones he found
in the garage of his rented home[1]

Now we come to a revealing twist in this tangled story. A US Marine—who should be a key witness, if US attorneys, the FBI, or congressmen on an oversight committee were looking for such an honest person to march into the drama—was thrust into this narrative.

Actually, what bought this retired Marine into the public eye was that he was deeply bothered by Rep. Debbie Wasserman Schultz's first and only defense of Imran and Hina Alvi Awan.

The congresswoman pointed a judgmental finger at anyone asking questions about the Awans and accused them of "ethnic and religious profiling."[2]

This US Marine thought that political tactic to be an insult to anyone who has ever run smack into the judgmental bite of discrimination in America.

And the congresswoman was playing the racial-profiling card loud.

"The right-wing media circus fringe has immediately focused not on this run-of-the-mill investigation just reporting the facts, but jumped to outrageous, egregious conclusions that they were trying to, that they have ties to terrorists and that they were stealing data," Representative Wasserman Schultz told her hometown newspaper. [3]

Imran's attorney, Chris Gowen, also used this call-the-messengers-racists defense. He said, "The attacks on Mr. Awan and his family began as part of a frenzy of anti-Muslim bigotry in the literal heart of our democracy, the House of Representatives."

Surely, Gowen and Wasserman Schultz are aware that crying racism in today's political debates is a conversation stopper. Suddenly, whoever is being accused of racism has been smeared with something that must be washed off with a strong defense, as they are guilty in the mainstream media until proven otherwise. The real questions, therefore, cease as the conversation turns to self-defense. This is why this tactic can be effective. If there is a weakness to this political maneuver, however, it's that some Democrats use it with such reckless abandon that their accusations start to ring like McCarthyism.

Such is why this retired Marine, Andre Taggart, spoke up. He had been pulled into this case by happenstance and only started speaking to the press because of this call-them-racists defense.

Taggart, you see, happens to be a black man, a lifelong Democrat, and, more importantly in regard to this criminal ring, a man who spent fourteen years in the United States Marine Corps. When he heard Wasserman Schultz's defense, he came forward to say this isn't a partisan or a racial issue but one about criminal activity. His personal experience with Imran Awan showed him that the Awans' religion and ethnicity wasn't what got them in such legal trouble. He contacted the *Daily Caller* to give his side of the story and spoke to other media members.

The simple story he told begins when he rented a home from Imran in mid-February 2017, just after Imran had been tossed off the congressional system on February 2. Taggart found the property on MilitaryByOwner.com, which made him assume Imran had some connection to the US military. When he rented the place and moved in with his family, however, Taggart didn't know he was dealing with

Imran Awan, because when they met, Imran had told Taggart his name was "Alex."

Taggart didn't know that Imran, his wife, brothers, and the rest of their team had just been fired after Imran provided false evidence to Capitol Police. By this time only a few members of Congress were still employing them. One was, of course, Representative Wasserman Schultz, but at this time Imran or Hina Alvi was also still working for Rep. Gregory Meeks (D-NY) and Rep. Marcia Fudge (D-OH)—though both would fire the Awans in the coming weeks.

"We moved in right after them," said Taggart. "They left a lot of items in the house. It seemed like they were moving out in a hurry. They told us they had a family tragedy. Considering how we found them through the website MilitaryByOwner.com, I had no reason to suspect them." Actually, Taggart assumed "Alex" (Imran) was former military.

In his hasty move, Imran had left a lot of furniture, appliances, and other items in the house. Taggart bought some of these items from Imran, but it was weeks before Taggart got around to looking in the garage and found what he called "government-issued computer equipment" that Imran had left behind.

Taggart says that soon after he moved in, he received a certified letter from the US House of Representatives. "They said they were ITs that worked for Congress, so I signed for it," says Taggart. "He seemed like a decent dude—wife, couple of kids. He seemed like he was hitting some adversity and he had to make an adjustment.... I tried to get [the letter] to them, and they wigged out on us. 'Oh, you shouldn't have signed for the letter.'...He was an asshole to me after that. I'm nice to everybody until they give me a reason not to."

After this interaction, Taggart decided to see what else was in the house he'd rented. That's when he found what looked like government bar codes on a lot of computer equipment in the garage. Taggart had spent a good portion of his fourteen years in the Marine Corps working as an avionics technician. He is now using this background to become an electrician, as he left the Marines in 2015. This background, experience, and his *Semper Fidelis* ("always faithful") training told him not to touch the computer equipment but to call the authorities instead.

Taggart, true to his casting, is a very plainspoken sort of guy. He says when he was active duty in the Marines, he often dealt with government-issued computer equipment and that the bar codes and other markings on the items in his garage made it clear to him the BlackBerries, laptops, and other items were the property of the US government. "Man, this looks like government-issued equipment," he recalls thinking. "Government equipment has certain markings on it. A lot of it was still manufacturer-sealed...and had government-issue bar codes on the boxes." When asked why he decided to call the authorities, he said his training had taught him to "take charge of all government equipment in view."

The authorities (Taggart is not certain which agency they were from) soon came and confiscated the equipment. Taggart, however, believes the FBI now has the equipment and says that after speaking with the FBI, he became aware agents had spent months watching his house and even watched him move in.

He says he didn't do a comprehensive count of the items he found in the garage. "I didn't count and lay it all out and inventory them... [but there were] maybe twenty pieces of equipment. Maybe four or five laptops, at least three or four BlackBerries," said Taggart. "I barely wanted to touch them. Government equipment—don't touch it, just turn it in. Don't turn it on, just turn it in."

Later, after the authorities had removed the computer equipment (some of which Taggart said was still in its original boxes, while other items looked used), he found out that the person he was renting from was actually Imran Awan, not "Alex."

He became aware of this thanks to George Webb, the person *The New York Times* called "a prolific right-wing YouTube conspiracy theorist"[4] but who is actually a Democrat and onetime volunteer for Sen. Bernie Sanders's 2016 campaign for president. Webb knocked on Taggart's door and they spoke. Taggart says he appreciated the information Webb gave him about Imran, but his impression was that Webb was sort of a conspiracy nut.

Still, Webb gave him a name to check out. After speaking with Webb, Taggart did some more research and became angry that Imran had lied to him about his real identity.

After he found out "Alex" was really Imran, he said, "I pulled up the lease and only saw Hina's name on there...that was the 'oh shit.'... Why didn't he tell me his real name? So I confronted him on his real name and he was real evasive. So I did my research and found out he was, you know, fired from Congress for stealing IT equipment."

Now Taggart realized he and his family had been duped into playing a part in a criminal investigation. "Once I found out what he was fired for, then I knew he intentionally misled me," he said. "That pissed me off—so now, you know, I'm gonna be an asshole when I see him."

Soon Taggart found out "Alex" had been under surveillance and authorities had been watching the house he'd rented from February through May 2017. He didn't like that Imran had put his family in this situation.

This had gotten personal. "He crossed me as a man," said Taggart. He also didn't like that Wasserman Schultz and Imran's attorney were blaming the investigation on anti-Muslim bigotry. He said, "How in the hell do four [Pakistani] nationals gain access through IT positions to the highest levels in Congress? How is it they got those jobs over equally qualified American citizens?"

As a Marine, Taggart wonders about Congress's vetting of IT aides. "I don't want to sound like a bigot or anything, I'm not, but an American citizen can be vetted all the way down to kindergarten.... Regardless of what you look like...common sense would be to hire Americans for these jobs."

The bigger political picture also bothered Taggart. He told the *Daily Caller* he believes it's unfair that the media is focusing so much on Trump and his alleged Russian connections but isn't mentioning Representative Wasserman Schultz and the Awans very much. "I see what's going on in the media," said Taggart. "I'd like to see that crook go to jail."

When asked about the media interest in the story, Taggart said, "The *Washington Post* called [but] didn't do a story." He also said he is ready and willing to tell US attorneys what he knows.

Given Taggart's nature, it's hardly surprising that the *Washington Post* decided not to run an article based on what he has to say—he certainly isn't following the Democrats' narrative on this case.

"Him, his wife, his brother, all working down there—there's no way they could do this without help. If we can drag Trump and his wingnuts through the mud for the Russia influence that they are having, then it's only fair that we also expose this shit," Taggart told the *Daily Caller*.

Taggart would later say he was probably a little worked up when he made the "wingnuts" comment, but he was upset that Representative Wasserman Schultz was using Islamophobia as cover. "Islamophobia is happening in this country. It is. And there is a lot of racism, bigotry, and overall hatred being disguised as patriotism in this country by the same people who are waving the flags that have nothing to do with the principles of this country that they claim to love so much, so there is that. And I acknowledge that. But this situation hasn't got a... thing to do with that. Nothing....These people are no-shit crooks in my opinion. They would do anything for money. I don't care that they're Muslim.... It's not Islamophobia to call out someone on their bullshit." [5]

Given Taggart's no-BS manner, it would be a refreshing event to hear him speak—without the profanity, of course—before a congressional committee investigating this case. Right there before the American people would be a down-to-earth, plainspoken retired US Marine telling them how it is from firsthand experience. Such a voice would help put this case in context for the public. Of course, that might be too honest a narrative for the *Washington Post* and other left-leaning media outlets to stomach, given that this case only involves Democrats.

Here's another taste of Taggart's perspective: "First of all, I am a black man in this country, so if you think I am unaware with how disgusting this climate is...I see it...acknowledging that something exists and letting it stifle you are two totally different things.... We are the same...race is a man-made invention in order for one group to establish dominance over the other.... If you don't want anyone to see your dirty emails, then stop putting people in you can't fully vet."

When asked about his straightforward manner, Taggart said, "You don't stop being a Marine 'cause you get out." But then, when asked if he thinks the Awans might have connections back in Pakistan or elsewhere where they might have sold some of the data they were harvesting from congressmen, he said, "I don't deal in speculation."

That's an honest, if gruff, *Semper Fi* point of view. Taggart clearly insists on following the rules of an honorable human being. Instead of speculating, he adheres to the dogmatic idea that we should not jump to conclusions but just follow the facts. Surely that's an approach to life more journalists should follow.

On September 1, 2017, Imran did try to get revenge. He had a lawyer, Jesse Winograd, another partner at Gowen Rhoades Winograd & Silva PLLC, send a letter to Taggart demanding $3,500 to fix drywall, $950 to refinish a hardwood floor, $7,000 to replace a carpet damaged by pets, and many more thousands of dollars for drawings made in crayon by Taggart's kids, ketchup stains, and more.[6]

Interestingly, the letter doesn't mention the many missing smartphones and computers the authorities confiscated after Taggart called the authorities. That would be admitting guilt, but the thoroughness and exorbitant amounts listed in the letter do say something about Imran's character—and maybe a little about a law firm that would represent him.

Meanwhile, a stubbornly honorable, if at times raw, person like Taggart should remind us to continually check our premises and not simply believe what we are told, and to follow what we think is in our best interest. The *Washington Post* reporter who called Taggart couldn't do that—or maybe their editor wouldn't.

As evidence has mounted, the many Democrats who paid the Awans have refrained from expressing alarm at the data the Awans might have or the many crimes they may have committed. Instead, they've either tried to ignore this case, downplay it, or make the claim that the investigation is a product of Islamophobia.

The problem is even a few Muslims who know Imran have begged to differ. Samina Gilani, the Awan brothers' stepmother, for example, complained to Virginia police that the Awans secretly bugged her home. She says that Imran claimed to be a "very powerful" employee working for congressmen, so influential he could order her family members in Pakistan to be kidnapped or even harm her relatives who live in the United States.

Imran even allegedly, according to Taggart, threatened to sue him to get back the computer equipment left in the garage of the home he rented; nevertheless, Taggart chose to alert the authorities and give it to them instead. Taggart clearly isn't a man who is afraid to do what is right, even if there might be consequences for doing the right thing.

For this reason, Taggart thought it "amazing" that Representative Wasserman Schultz dared suggest Imran was a victim of religious discrimination. "It pisses me off," said Taggart. By doing this, he said, Wasserman Schultz is diminishing real acts of discrimination. And, as she is doing this, she knows full well she exposed herself and Congress to an insider threat.

Taggart's thoughts about what should happen to Wasserman Schultz are just as plain. "The people who facilitated them should also be locked up, as far as I'm concerned," he said.

Honest declarations like that from a former US Marine who dealt directly with Imran could clearly be publicly damaging to Representative Wasserman Schultz and the other Democrats who employed the Awans. The *Daily Caller* even reported: "Senior congressional officials called [Wasserman Schultz's] lack of cooperation 'unsettling,' and suggested the results of the investigation could very well lead to her resignation."

Forcing resignations over this case would take a lot more media attention. That could have happened if US attorneys had pressed the case beyond the bank fraud Imran and Hina Alvi were indicted for in the summer of 2017. Still, it does seem obvious that part of the reason these Democrats were willing to overlook apparent problems was because their former aides are Muslims and first-generation immigrants, a class of people treated as victims in need of protection by many Democrats.

Identity politics can place a politically correct blindfold on a politician. Such a view can even suppress common sense; for example, condemning or preventing law enforcement agencies from focusing on young Muslim men from specific regions of certain countries with known ties to terrorist organizations is nonsensical political correctness in action. Surely, individuals are innocent until proven guilty and therefore can't be punished unless convicted by a court of law, but this doesn't or shouldn't mean law enforcement can't focus on people who are statistically much more likely to commit certain crimes.

Taggart, in contrast, speaks like an American who has backbone and his eyes open. He sees racism and condemns it, but he still saw enough goodness in this country to join the US Marines, to proudly serve, and to insist that the values he lived by in the service be upheld by Congress. After all, if a Marine, whatever his or her skin color or religion, upholds the standards of the Corps, they are (or should be) rewarded. Meanwhile, discrimination shouldn't be tolerated, as discriminating against someone because of their ethnicity, religion, or another factor is a direct affront to the body of law built on the US Constitution, particularly its first ten amendments known as the Bill of Rights. Justice is supposed to be blind, and we are all equal under the law. That certainly isn't how the system always works, but that is the dream worth fighting for that Taggart and men and women like him exemplify.

In stark contrast, given Representative Wasserman Schultz's defense of Imran and Hina Alvi, it's hard to imagine that her judgment wasn't clouded by her view that the Awans are part of a protected class of people.

Former California congressman Xavier Becerra is another person who employed the Awans and seems to see them as members of a politically protected class of immigrants. Becerra is now the attorney general of California. He self-identifies as a person from a protected class of Mexican immigrants. He often begins speeches by telling people he is a second-generation immigrant, as his mother was born in Jalisco, Mexico. She moved to America after marrying his father. Becerra was one of Imran's first employers in the House of Representatives and looked the other way for years as the Awans did strange and illegal things on the House Democratic Caucus server, a caucus Becerra chaired.

Becerra often describes the world in terms of his views of race. "I certainly believe...that [president Donald J. Trump is] a bigoted man," said Becerra. "I certainly believe that if he's unwilling to say he apologizes for the racist things that he's said, that he should be classified as a racist."[7]

Many other Democrats have shown that their brand of identity politics has also colored how they see this case. Rep. Gregory Meeks said he was hesitant to believe the accusations against Hina Alvi and Imran Awan because of their ethnicity. "I wanted to be sure individuals are not being singled out because of their nationalities or their religion. We want to make sure everybody is entitled to due process," Meeks said. "They had provided great service for me. And there were certain times in which they had permission by me, if it was Hina or someone else, to access some of my data."[8]

Representative Meeks has been consistent about this belief. His former chief of staff, Jameel Aalim-Johnson, is an American convert to Islam and was a cofounder of the Congressional Muslim Staff Association (CMSA), an organization that brought a lot of controversial figures to Capitol Hill to lead prayer sessions. This included Anwar al-Awlaki,[9] the Muslim cleric and US citizen who recruited for al-Qaeda and who hid in Yemen before being killed by a US drone strike in that country in 2011.

Aalim-Johnson also participated in a July 19, 2004, Summer Leadership Conference at the embassy of Pakistan. The theme of the conference was "Young Americans of Pakistani Heritage Working to Build a Better America." This conference focused on encouraging young Pakistani-Americans to pursue careers on Capitol Hill and sought to create a network of such politically oriented Pakistani-Americans.[10]

There is a photo from the conference that shows Aalim-Johnson sitting next to Randall "Ismail" Royer, a former communications associate for the Council on American-Islamic Relations, who confessed in 2004 to receiving jihadist training in Pakistan and who was sentenced to a twenty-year prison term. The Pakistani jihadist group Royer trained with is Lashkar-e-Taiba, which is well known as an instrument of Pakistan's Inter-Services Intelligence (ISI), its premier intelligence agency. Lashkar-e-Taiba was originally funded by Osama bin Laden. Royer would spend fourteen years in prison in a cell alongside people like Terry Nichols, who was an accomplice in the Oklahoma City bombing; Eric Rudolph who bombed abortion clinics and the Atlanta Olympics; and Richard Reid, who is known as the "shoe bomber." Since his release from prison, Royer, however, has been working against religious extremism.[11]

Anwar Hajjaj, an Islamic cleric, was another controversial figure who led prayer sessions for the CMSA in a congressional building. Hajjaj headed the Taibah International Aid Association, which was designated a global terrorist organization by the US Treasury Department in May 2004. He also served as director of the World Assembly of Muslim Youth (WAMY) headed by Osama bin Laden's nephew, Abdullah bin Laden, who left the country when WAMY offices were raided by the FBI in June 2004. Hajjaj was also president of Dar Al-Hijrah Islamic Center, a mosque in Falls Church, Virginia, where al-Awlaki served as imam and where at least two of the 9/11 hijackers attended services. Hajjaj, according to sources, even asked Rep. Gregory Meeks to intervene on his behalf with the Department of Homeland Security for what he said was harassment he received when he returned to the United States from trips to Saudi Arabia. At the time, Representative Meeks said he was asked to intervene by a mutual acquaintance—this was Jameel Aalim-Johnson.[12]

It's unclear if Imran Awan, his wife, or his brothers attended these CMSA prayer sessions and so heard Anwar al-Awlaki or Anwar Hajjaj speak in a room in the Rayburn House Office Building, as the two cofounders of the CMSA, Jameel Aalim-Johnson and Assad Akhter, a Pakistani-American and former deputy chief of staff for Rep. Bill Pascrell Jr. (D-NJ), both declined media requests for this book. Also, none of this is related here to make any claim that Representative Meeks or Jameel Aalim-Johnson condone the actions of or support terrorists in any way; rather, it is recounted to point out how much political correctness can warp someone's judgment.

Representative Meeks is certainly correct that due process is an American right Imran Awan is protected by, but this doesn't mean that Congress, or any employer, shouldn't at least suspend an employee who is under investigation for being the type of insider threat Imran Awan was.

The fact that these members of Congress, and perhaps some of their staffers, let political correctness cloud their judgment certainly is part of the story. It can't, however, be the entire story, as it would take a blind fool to miss all the signs from these individuals in this insider-threat scenario.

We know that everyone the Awans came in contact with didn't miss the signs, as many congressional staffers have expressed concern and outrage over the odd loyalty some members of Congress showed for this group of IT aides. Congressmen had also been warned about insider threats, such as the Awans were, as early as 2008 by internal reviews done by the House inspector general.

Still, even all that is only the beginning, because a lot of other evidence points to something much bigger than fraud and theft. Imran and his crew were also clearly behaving as spies.

CHAPTER 6

SPIES IN CONGRESS

The iPhones officially assigned to House staffers had Imran Awan's email address listed as the phones' Apple IDs. The only reason I can think of for why Imran would do that is this would have given him the ability to see everything these staffers were doing.

—House IT aide with more than a decade of experience working for congressmen

I say, "Just tell me how it is, Clare. You're ex-CIA; you're a highly regarded expert on the Middle East. Why do you say Imran Awan and his team were spies?"

Clare Lopez smiles and leans over a small, round table in a popular Washington restaurant. She has yet to take a bite of her salad. She has too much to say.

"Because they clearly acted as spies," she says plainly, as if it couldn't be anything else. "They were copying all of those congressmen's data, reams of it. Why? They gave the authorities a fake copy of those servers. Why? They allegedly destroyed computer equipment the FBI wanted. They spent a lot of time in Pakistan even as they worked for Congress. What were they doing? They are dual citizens. They

133

are from Pakistan. These aren't loyal American patriots. They acted secretively. They were paid exorbitant salaries. They were involved in other businesses, including a car dealership that was very shady—car dealerships are favorite fronts for international money laundering.

"I say they are spies because this has all the signs of an ISI, ah Pakistani intelligence, cell in Congress. It's the only way it adds up."[1]

I wanted Clare Lopez to unpack all that, as she has deep experience in the Middle East with the CIA and today is vice president for research and analysis at the Center for Security Policy, a DC-based think tank. Actually, her résumé reads like the profile of a composite character made up by Robert Ludlum.

After getting a BA in communications and French from Notre Dame College in Ohio and an MA in international relations from the Maxwell School of Syracuse University, she completed Marine Corps Officer Candidate School in Quantico, Virginia, but then declined a military commission so she could join the Central Intelligence Agency as a career operations officer.

In February 2012, Lopez was named a member of the Task Force on National and Homeland Security, which focuses on the electromagnetic pulse (EMP) threat to the nation. She has been a guest lecturer on counterterrorism, national defense, and international relations at Georgetown University. Since 2013, she has served as a member of the Citizens' Commission on Benghazi. She has been hired as a consultant, intelligence analyst, and researcher for a variety of defense firms. She was named a 2011 Lincoln Fellow at the Claremont Institute. She is the coauthor of two books on Iran—*Gulen and the Gulenist Movement* and *See No Shariah: Countering Violent Extremism and the Disarming of America's First Line of Defense*.

"A lot of sources have said what you're saying in different ways," I say, "but why do you seem so sure?"

"Because people who grew up in Pakistan, like Imran Awan, don't look at the US as home," says Clare. "Pakistan is home. In tribal Pakistan they have allegiances to family and clan. He came to the US, thanks to our visa lottery, at seventeen years old, plenty old enough to be indoctrinated first. Omar Mateen, the mass murderer who killed forty-nine people at the Pulse nightclub in Orlando, Florida, in 2016, was raised in the US by Afghan parents but still radicalized and identified himself as an Islamic soldier to police during his terrorist attack.

"So yeah, by seventeen I'd say Imran was pretty well cooked," says Lopez candidly, amid the noise of a bustling restaurant, with cold January air whooshing in every time someone opens the door.

"The Awans were clearly a cell," she says. "They were likely doing espionage. Pakistan is very interested in the US Congress—where members stand, how they'll vote, and so on—for a variety of reasons. The Awans might have even been blackmailing congressmen, I don't know. As a longtime analyst for the CIA, I can tell you the Awans were clearly behaving as spies. Maybe that's why so few people want to talk about this."

Now I have to ask, "So, in your experience, the US intelligence community would want this hushed up?"

"Absolutely," says Clare. "Right now, Pakistan basically has the troops we have in Afghanistan hostage, as the supply routes go through Pakistan."

Lopez takes a bite of the salmon topping on her salad. As she pauses, I ask if what we know about what the Awans did in Congress fits with how Pakistani intelligence agencies behave.

She nods and says, "Pakistan is a jihadi state. They are not our friend. They are actually closer to China than to us. They cooperate to some extent with us because it benefits them, but they are not our ally.

"And yes, this kind of plot is typical of how ISI works. The Awans were very likely recruited by the ISI," says Lopez.

Imran Awan's well-established greed would have certainly made him susceptible to be turned into a spy. His long stays in Pakistan, his business ties to a controversial land there,[2] payments to the Pakistani police that news reports in Pakistan refer to and that even Imran's lawyer confirmed, the data he was copying from members Congress—all of this evidence makes him sound like a cliché of a bad spy character. But I ask if the ISI would really be interested in a man like Imran Awan.

"He was an ideal tool for the ISI. And ISI has a habit of contacting, even threatening, Pakistanis in the US," says Lopez.

Again, Inter-Services Intelligence is Pakistan's premier intelligence agency. The ISI is operationally responsible for gathering, processing, and analyzing national security information from around the world. The ISI reports to the director general of Pakistan and is mostly staffed with military officers drawn on the branches of their armed services—hence the name "Inter-Services." The ISI gained global recognition in the 1980s when it supported the Afghan mujahideen against the Soviet Union during the Soviet-Afghan War. During that war, the ISI did work in close coordination with the CIA to train and support the mujahideen with American, Pakistani, and Saudi funds, as it then benefited them to do so monetarily and they didn't want the Soviet Union to move on to Pakistan next.

After the fall of the Soviet Union, however, the ISI provided strategic support and intelligence to the Afghan Taliban fighting against the Northern Alliance during a civil war in Afghanistan in the 1990s. The Northern Alliance became the chief US ally when, after the September 11, 2001, terrorist attacks, the United States moved to overthrow the Taliban's terrorist state in Afghanistan. So the United States, for practical reasons, actually needed to be friendly with elements of both sides of combatants in a recent civil war. Given this situation, it's hardly surprising that Pakistan, which had supported the Taliban openly, would work with the United States while at the same time giving the Taliban as much safe haven as they could get away with inside Pakistan.

Part of the reason Pakistan does this is because there is a lot of anti-American sentiment in the country. In fact, many analysts point out that Pakistan often finds it useful to play up or even stoke anti-American feelings among its citizens. This is part of the reason why Pakistan has too often supported or overlooked schools designed to indoctrinate children in the Islamic extremism aligned with Taliban interests.

"Anti-American sentiment is higher in Pakistan than most Americans realize and most American officials are willing to acknowledge. That sentiment is also visible in the behavior of the Pakistani government," said Lawrence Sellin,[3] a former US Army colonel who served in Afghanistan and Iraq but who was controversially removed from his post as a staff officer at the International Security Assistance Force Joint Command (ISAF) in Kabul after he criticized the US Army's overreliance on PowerPoint slide presentations in an opinion piece published by United Press International. Sellin had written that the ISAF's command structure, which coordinates the day-to-day war effort, was nothing more than "endless tinkering with PowerPoint slides to conform with the idiosyncrasies of cognitively challenged generals in order to spoon-feed them information."

Sellin, though he broke NATO Directive 95-1, meaning he failed to clear "written or oral presentations to the media" through a designated public affairs officer, certainly proved himself to be a truth teller who is unafraid of political correctness.

Clare Lopez agrees with Sellin's assessment of Pakistan and that some light needs to be shined on its motivations, anti-American sentiment, and extremism.

For perspective, Lopez mentions a 2011 incident in Lahore, Pakistan (very near Imran Awan's home town of Faisalabad), that exposed the complicated relationship between the US and Pakistan spy agencies. This occurred when a CIA contractor named Raymond Davis killed two men after, he says, they pulled a gun on him.

On January 27, 2011, Davis was driving alone in a white Honda Civic when he stopped at a traffic light in the Mozang Chungi area of Lahore. In a written statement, Davis said two men pulled alongside him on a motorbike. One of the men, he said, brandished a pistol. Davis reacted by drawing his 9mm Glock pistol and killing them both.

Davis was arrested and charged with murder. The ISI and the CIA worked closely together during the 1980s Afghan war, but after the withdrawal of Soviet troops from Afghanistan, the relationship between the two spy agencies became more troubled as they pursued different interests and beliefs. The September 11, 2001, attacks in the United States and the subsequent US invasion of Afghanistan to overthrow the Taliban created a new and more complex relationship. The dynamics of the CIA-ISI partnership were quite different after 9/11, as Pakistan's then-military dictator, Pervez Musharraf, didn't seriously

FRANK MINITER

try to root out al-Qaeda and Taliban forces in Pakistan, even though he said he would.

So Davis was caught in the contradictions of these complex differences between a nation that didn't want to see terrorists from the region revisit its doorstep and a nation that found such radicalism useful.

Davis would spend seven weeks in a Pakistani jail as his case triggered a serious diplomatic crisis between Islamabad and Washington. Religious groups in Pakistan at the time were demanding the death penalty for Davis. Public opinion in Pakistan, which as was noted can be very anti-American, also favored trying Davis for murder.

But then, all of a sudden, Davis was freed. What happened was American interests used the Islamic law of *diya* (blood money for the victims' families) to free Davis. Essentially, millions of dollars was paid to the relatives of the men who'd drawn the gun on him.

In his memoir, *The Contractor: How I Landed in a Pakistani Prison and Ignited a Diplomatic Crisis*, Davis claims the ISI helped to orchestrate his exit—a fact Pakistani media wasn't free enough to report.

"Several guards led me out of the courtroom through a back entrance," writes Davis. "One of the men opened the door, stepped out into a courtyard, and scanned the horizon...once he'd cleared the area, I was waved through the door and directed to the SUV idling in the courtyard."

"Certainly you score points in the court of public opinion when you cater to Pakistan's widespread anti-Americanism," Michael Kugelman, Asia Program deputy director and senior associate for South Asia at the Washington-based Woodrow Wilson International Center for Scholars, told the German news service DW. "At the same time, the ISI was genuinely furious with the CIA after the Davis affair, and many CIA personnel were effectively expelled from Pakistan. The CIA presence today hasn't come close to approaching its levels from before the Davis affair."[4]

Months later, the raid by US Navy SEALs in the Pakistani city of Abbottabad on May 2, 2011, to capture or kill the al-Qaeda leader Osama bin Laden brought the troubled CIA-ISI relationship to the brink of collapse.

After the raid, five Pakistanis who allegedly worked as informants for the CIA to pass information that led to the death of Osama bin Laden, thanks to bullets fired by Navy SEALs, were arrested by the ISI. After they were arrested, the United States expended a lot of diplomacy in a failed attempt to get one of them, Shakil Afridi, a Pakistani physician, released. Afridi ran a fake vaccination campaign that provided critical intelligence for the raid on the Osama bin Laden compound. But the Pakistani government refused to release Afridi, who has since been serving a thirty-three-year prison sentence for helping America make Osama bin Laden pay for his heinous crimes.

This anti-American climate is what Imran Awan and the relatives who followed him to the United States grew up in. It is what they reentered when they went back for months-long stays in Pakistan even as they worked for dozens of members of the US Congress—stints where they reportedly worked remotely by logging on to Congress's computer system from Pakistan.

While Imran was working as an IT administrator for various members of Congress and, from May 4, 2011, to July 28, 2016, for Rep. Debbie Wasserman Schultz as she ran the Democratic National Committee, the ISI was pushing back against the CIA presence in Pakistan and doing counterintelligence work in the United States. Actually, in the aftermath of the shooting involving CIA contractor Raymond Davis, the ISI became more serious about curbing American spy agency work. During this time, at "least 30 suspected covert American operatives have suspended their activities in Pakistan and 12 have reportedly left the country."[5]

Meanwhile, the US government was also taking Pakistan's spies in the United States more seriously. In 2011, a Chinese woman believed to be an ISI agent who headed the Chinese unit of a US manufacturer was charged with illegally exporting high-performance coatings to be used in Pakistan's nuclear power plants. Xun Wang, a former managing director of PPG Paints Trading in Shanghai, a Chinese subsidiary of United States–based PPG Industries Inc., was indicted on a charge of conspiring to violate the International Emergency Economic Powers Act and related offenses. Wang was accused of conspiring to export and re-export high-performance epoxy coatings to the Chashma 2 Nuclear Power Plant in Pakistan.

A year earlier, an ISI operative named Mohammed Tasleem, an attaché in Pakistan's New York consulate, was accused of issuing threats against Pakistanis living in the United States. Tasleem was allegedly doing this to prevent Pakistanis from speaking openly about Pakistan's government.

A *New York Times* story in July 2011 reported on the FBI's hunt for the Pakistani spy:[6]

> F.B.I. agents hunting for Pakistani spies in the United States last year began tracking Mohammed Tasleem, an attaché in the Pakistani Consulate in New York and a clandestine operative of Pakistan's military spy agency, the Directorate for Inter-Services Intelligence.
>
> Mr. Tasleem, they discovered, had been posing as an F.B.I. agent to extract information from Pakistanis living in the United States and was issuing threats to keep them from speaking openly about Pakistan's government. His activities were part of what government officials in Washington, along with a range of Pakistani journalists and scholars, say is a systematic ISI campaign to keep tabs on the Pakistani diaspora inside the United States.
>
> The F.B.I. brought Mr. Tasleem's activities to Leon E. Panetta, then the director of the Central Intelligence Agency, and last April, Mr. Panetta had a tense conversation with Pakistan's spymaster, Lt. Gen. Ahmed Shuja Pasha.
>
> Within days, Mr. Tasleem was spirited out of the United States—a quiet resolution typical of the spy games among the world's powers.
>
> But some of the secrets of that hidden world became public last week when two Pakistani-

Americans working for a charity that the F.B.I. believes is a front for Pakistan's spy service were indicted. Only one was arrested; the other is still in Pakistan.

The investigation exposed one part of what American officials say is a broader campaign by the Pakistani spy agency, known as the ISI, to exert influence over lawmakers, stifle public dialogue critical of Pakistan's military and blunt the influence of India, Pakistan's longtime adversary.

Clare Lopez explains that the ISI is widely feared inside Pakistan because of these tactics. American intelligence officials believe, for example, that some ISI operatives ordered the killing of Pakistani journalist Saleem Shahzad. At the same time, the ISI remains a partner of the CIA in the hunt for al-Qaeda, and Pakistan controls the routes into Afghanistan needed to supply American troops there. This complex relationship often makes it difficult for the United States to put pressure on Pakistan.

"The ISI guys will look into your eyes and will indirectly threaten you by introducing themselves," reported *The New York Times*. "The ISI makes sure that they are present in every occasion relating to Pakistan, and in some cases, they pay ordinary Pakistanis for attending events and pass them information."[7]

Given the ISI's habit of visiting Pakistanis who live in America to "exert influence over lawmakers [and] stifle public dialogue critical of Pakistan's military," as *The New York Times* put it, it would actually be odd, even out of character, for the ISI not to have contacted the Awans.

Reporting by Luke Rosiak of the *Daily Caller*, and Wajid Ali Syed, a correspondent with Pakistan's Geo TV in Washington, turned up a firsthand witness in Pakistan who says Imran Awan was supplying information to the ISI.

An ex-business partner, Rashid Minhas, of Imran Awan's late father, Haji Ashraf Awan, told the *Daily Caller* that Imran's father was giving data to a Pakistani official named Rehman Malik. Minhas even says Imran had bragged that he had so much power in Congress he could "change the U.S. president."

When Minhas was asked how he knew this, he reportedly said that in 2008, his brother, Abdul Razzaq, saw a "USB given to Rehman Malik by Imran's father."[8]

Minhas even said that after Imran Awan's father had delivered a USB drive to Malik, four ISI agents then acted as bodyguards for him. Minhas didn't tell the *Daily Caller* what was on the USB; it's unclear if he knew. Like so many other witnesses to the Awan's likely criminal enterprise and possible international spy cell, Minhas said he has not been approached by US intelligence agencies to give information about this or other events about which he may have firsthand knowledge.

Congressional investigators also came to the conclusion that Imran and his relatives behaved as spies after Imran was arrested trying to fly to Pakistan in July 2017. An internal report by the House Office of Inspector General in the late summer of 2017 concluded that the Awans had made unauthorized access to congressional servers in 2016, allegedly accessed data of members of Congress they didn't work for, logged in as members of Congress themselves, and attempted to cover their tracks by providing false data, stealing a server, and destroying computer hardware. This is all according to a presentation summarizing the findings of the House inspector general's four-month internal probe.

The summary said the Awans' behavior mirrored a "classic method for insiders to exfiltrate data from an organization." It also said the Awans continued even after they were told to stop accessing a server for the House Democratic Caucus and that there are indications data belonging to numerous congressmen was likely copied to a server the members of Congress didn't control. House authorities say the entire server was subsequently stolen, as in physically taken. This would later be disputed by the Department of Justice in a plea-deal agreement they reached with Imran; nevertheless, the agreement doesn't bring in new evidence to counter the House IG report.

"Clearly they were acting as spies," says Lopez, who at the time wasn't aware of many of the details insiders in Congress have given for this book.

Incredibly, when members of Congress who employed this team of IT administrators from Pakistan were informed by the House IG about what the Awans had been up to, many of them turned around and misrepresented the crimes as nothing more than theft, not possible espionage. Perhaps they downplayed the situation to avoid paying a political price for having employed and overpaid an ISI spy ring.

The House Office of Inspector General presentation for members of Congress on the Awans' breech actually used the headline "UNAUTHORIZED ACCESS" for the summary report. The report says, "5 shared employee system administrators have collectively logged into 15 member offices and the Democratic Caucus although they were not employed by the offices they accessed."

The House IG also found that a House server was "being used for nefarious purposes and elevated the risk that individuals could be reading and/or removing information."

The server they referred to was that of the House Democratic Caucus, which at the time was run by Rep. Xavier Becerra of California. The "individuals" named were, of course, Imran Awan, his wife Hina Alvi, his brothers Abid and Jamal, and his friend Rao Abbas. Abid's wife, Natalia Soba, and Imran's friend Haseeb Rana weren't employed by members of Congress at the time of the House IG investigation.

The House inspector general's report also found that one of the IT aides "logged into a member's office two months after he was terminated from that office." Now, it's possible the rules could have been violated for some harmless reason, but the House IG didn't think that a likely explanation. It said in its summary presentation: "This pattern of login activity suggests steps are being taken to conceal their activity."

The House IG also found "possible storage of sensitive House information outside the House...Dropbox is installed on two Caucus computers used by the shared employees. Two user accounts had thousands of files in their Dropbox folder on each computer."

As was previously noted, using Dropbox is against House rules because it uploads files off-site—a place where House authorities can't protect members of Congress's data. The *Washington Post* had referenced this House IG presentation in July of 2017 and quoted a House source who claimed that the server was full of the Awans' children's "homework" and "family photos" to account for the terabytes of data being moved.[9] The IG presentation didn't find that to be a likely scenario: "Based on the file names, some of the information is likely sensitive," it says.

The IG summary presentation also says: "All 5 of the shared employee system administrators collectively logged onto the Caucus system 5,735 times, an average of 27 times per day.... This is considered unusual since computers in other offices managed by these shared employees were accessed in total less than 60 times."

This odd and constant access by the Awans certainly doesn't support the *Washington Post*'s assertion that Imran Awan, Hina Alvi, and the others were only using the Democratic Caucus server as a convenient place to store homework and family photos.

Interestingly, when Representative Becerra's House Democratic Caucus found out about the Awans' unusual activity and tried to stop them, according to the House IG presentation, the Awans continued to access the server anyway.

"The [Democratic] Caucus Chief of Staff requested one of the shared employees to not provide IT services or access their computers," the IG report says. "This shared employee continued."

Then, as Capitol Police were watching the server as a part of their investigation, they discovered in January of 2017 that it had been removed and replaced with a different server. Soon after, Capitol Police would demand an image (a copy of the contents) of the server but would be given a fake image (possibly of the new server, not the old one that had so much data from members of Congress on it).

For these and other reasons, Clare Lopez is convinced Imran Awan and his crew were spies, likely working for Pakistan's Inter-Services Intelligence.

Other experts agree with her analysis.

Another interview in a DC restaurant jumped to mind, and I wanted to ask Lopez about what this person had told me. In that interview, we sat in the restaurant's outdoor section a short walk from the Capitol Building. The day was warm, the sky blue, and it was just after one o'clock on a Wednesday in October. The man who sat across from me at the small metal table had spent his life in intelligence, but, like so many of his type, he doesn't want his name in print.

Before we met, he was very up front with the fact that he had nothing specific to tell me about Imran Awan and his crew. I wanted to meet him anyway because he did have something important to say about how the Awans were able to play the system so easily.

Because he'd spent many years in the region, we first talked about Pakistan and Middle Eastern politics, the growing Russian influence in the region, and all the complications that area of the world brings with it. But he kept circling back to a point he wanted me to understand.

"Just know," he said, leaning across the table between us, "this case is not just a criminal matter that happens to have something to do with a group of people from Pakistan. Seeing it that way is too short-sighted. The whole strange drama is really about spies in Congress."

He sat back against the metal chair to let that sink in a moment. I pondered his perspective as people strolled by on the sidewalk to my left on the lovely autumn day. I'm not a journalist who's into conspiracy theories. I want the truth. I refuse to make big leaps from one dot to the next to force some convenient narrative together. He saw this cynicism in my expression and leaned back in, with his elbows on the table.

"Don't get me wrong," he said, with his hands clasped together and his voice clear and slow, "they also sound like criminals to me. But much of what they did was also spying. I'm not saying they were directly working for some foreign intelligence service. They may have been, but they might have also sold the data on the market—there are a lot of players who'd buy congressmen's emails and other revealing data for a lot of reasons, especially the ones the Awans worked for who were in leadership positions on the various committees."

As we spoke openly in the restaurant's outdoor section, it was hard not to find it amusing that, though this man asked for his name to be kept out of print, he didn't mind speaking with me in public. Such is Washington, which is so full of elected officials, the thousands on their staffs, the many more political appointees who run federal agencies, and those in positions of power in the White House, that only the most nationally recognizable people bother to change their behavior in public.

For this reason, it wasn't surprising to anyone who knows Washington that when a *New York Times* reporter overheard a conversation at the next table at BLT Steak, a downtown Washington steakhouse, between a then-White House attorney, Ty Cobb, and another attorney in September 2017. The two lawyers were openly discussing presidential privilege as it related to an investigation into possible collusion between the Trump campaign and Russia.[10] What was a little unusual was that the *Times* reporter sketched out the scene publicly in a column. It's more typical for reporters to use what they gather by eavesdropping at a bar or restaurant as background as they try to confirm quotes and facts with the parties or other sources.

"Seeing [the Awans and their crew] only as criminals restricts the investigation and misses the big picture," this source said. "Such a point of view misses the all-too-real threats. Seeing them as the spies they are, however, broadens the perspective and forces us to focus on the real threat: Congress has been wide open to these insider attacks. So have our intelligence agencies. The biggest intelligence failures have come from insiders like Edward Snowden, not from hackers."

He has a point. Looking at Imran Awan and his crew of congressional IT aides as simply a criminal ring is too narrow-minded. With that limited view, Capitol Police would investigate crimes and US attorneys would then look over the evidence to see if they should prosecute. Meanwhile, the House Office of Inspector General would fulfill its responsibilities by providing recommendations for improving the performance, accountability, and integrity of House financial, administrative, and technology-based operations.

Sources for this book have said that all of that has been occurring behind the scenes, as it should be. But if that's all that happens, then certainly investigators and congressmen will miss the bigger, more dangerous threat, which was what this intelligence expert was primarily worried about.

This source explained that it's not surprising few are saying the Awans behaved as spies. The State Department and/or US intelligence agencies likely don't want this case to include charges of spying, since a court case could reveal sources and methods. It could also embarrass Pakistan and thereby endanger US goals in that region. Such worries would be communicated to FBI agents on the case. As part of their responsibilities, these agents meet with the US attorneys charged with prosecuting a case. Certainly, US attorneys on a case such as this would be informed in higher-level meetings in the US Department of Justice that this situation is internationally sensitive—anything less would be a massive oversight by the various agencies. The DOJ, after all, oversees the FBI. The DOJ could ignore recommendations from the State Department or another part of the bureaucracy, but in this case, why would they? There has been little public pressure placed on them by the media. The thing is, only seeing the Awans as possible criminals misses the big picture about insider threats embedded in Congress, which could leave its members open to new attacks. A lot of evidence, after all, does show these particular IT administrators were clearly behaving as spies.

Still, a lot of pundits and members of Congress—particularly Democrats, as this case only involves Democrats in the House— would surely mock anyone who expresses this broader but critical distinction. It is politically advantageous for them if this investigation is only seen as a criminal matter, a case where the villains can be quietly punished for bank fraud as Congress updates security protocols. This way, the congressmen involved can quietly move on as if nothing really had happened.

So I threw this at Clare Lopez. "As I said, just give it to me straight: Would Congress, even the US intelligence community, purposely keep this from the American public, maybe to protect their sources or to prevent further worsening the US relationship with Pakistan?"

Lopez was nodding. "Yes, that's how they think."

Clearly, members of Congress don't want to pay a political price for allowing this group of IT administrators to run amuck in the halls of the House. Many Democrats, in Congress and the media, also don't want the narrative that the Russians are behind everything to be watered down or perhaps disproved by authorities or reporters who look into this case from that broader perspective—that would take pressure off the Trump administration before the 2018 midterm elections.

The trouble is, if politicians don't appreciate the size and scope of this threat, then Congress—and our democratic system—might be left with the gaping security holes that allowed the Awans to do all they did in the first place. The number-one security threat with any modern network is, after all, always the human element. If people aren't aware of the seriousness of this problem, they might not take security as seriously. This could leave Congress vulnerable to Russian interference in our democracy via the same tactics the Awans got away with for so long—to name one problem Democrats have been screaming about since Donald J. Trump won the presidential election in 2016.

If we also view the Awans as spies, however, we then must look around the world at the actors on the international stage who would, and perhaps did in this case, take advantage of these security holes in Congress and other parts of our democratic system.

Still, given the lack of honest media narrative with this case, it's understandable that many might at first think the word "spy" is too strong; after all, little information has gone public showing that the Awans sold the information they gathered to foreign intelligence agencies or other groups. But then, even the dictionary says the Awans acted as spies. As a noun, Dictionary.com gives four definitions for "spy." The first is a "person employed by a government to obtain secret information or intelligence about another, usually hostile, country, especially with reference to military or naval affairs." We don't yet know if Imran fits that definition. But the second definition of a spy is a person "who keeps close and secret watch on the actions and words of another or others." Imran certainly did that. He copied terabytes of information from the more than forty members of Congress he and his team worked for. He copied the information onto a server he controlled and then proceeded to, against House rules, log on to the server thousands of times. That's how a spy behaves.

And Imran was behaving as a spy when he, according to House documents revealed in a public hearing,[11] backed up data onto a private Dropbox account, even though doing so was against House rules.

Imran might have even kept copies of this data, as the House IG says the server in question disappeared and was replaced by another server. It isn't known, at least publicly, whether the authorities ever got their hands on this original House Democratic Caucus server. Even if they did, Imran could have easily backed up the files onto flash drives or other devices and hidden those devices as a sort of open-ended threat to any congressman he worked for, since all their incoming and outgoing emails and other data was in those files. Could this be why many of the members of Congress and their staffs are not outwardly helping authorities or even publicly condemning the Awans?

Even if these members of Congress did nothing wrong, there are sure to be embarrassing things in their emails. Some might have criticized other Democrats for votes they took or wouldn't take. There might be positions they took privately that are different from things they said publicly—a very normal thing for a politician to do as legislation is made. Maybe there are things in their emails and other files that could easily be taken out of context by their adversaries in upcoming primaries or the next election.

What normal person wouldn't be embarrassed or even harmed if all their private thoughts expressed in emails and/or texts went public?

These members of Congress must know that the Awans could do this to them; after all, even Imran's mother-in-law, Samina Gilani, claimed in a court filing in Fairfax, Virginia, that Imran was behaving as a spy. She said he had tapped her phone and that "some other recording devices were also installed/planted in my house at 6314 Thomas Drive, Springfield, VA.... Mr. Shahid Imran Awan did admit to me that my phone is taped and there are devices installed in the house to listen my all conversations and that he will remove all these devices."

Clearly Imran was adept at using the tools of a spy. And Imran did much more than allegedly spy on his mother-in-law.

Imran was even spying on congressional staffers.

Congressional Staffers Also Were Spied On

"Some of the IT administrators who've taken over the congressional offices Imran Awan did IT for told me the iPhones officially assigned to House staffers had Imran Awan's email address listed as the phones' Apple IDs. The only reason I can think of for why he would do that is this would have given him the ability to see everything these staffers were doing," said a House IT aide with more than a decade of experience working for congressmen.

An Apple ID is the account someone uses to access Apple services such as the App Store, Apple Music, iCloud, iMessage, and FaceTime. "It includes the email address and password you use to sign in as well as all the contact, payment, and security details you'll use across Apple services," says Apple.

IT aides interviewed for this book were shocked to find that Imran had used his own email address as the Apple ID for staffers' iPhones. This would have given Imran access to all the texts these staffers were sending, all the data they had in iCloud, possibly their personal credit card numbers, their emails, and more. House IT administrators found this out soon after the Awans were booted off the House computer system on February 2, 2017.

This isn't how House IT administrators—or even those who work for private companies—behave. This is how a spy behaves.

The House IT administrators spoken to for this book all said the Awans were a secretive and elusive bunch. It's actually normal for these IT professionals to speak to each other. IT aides in Congress often have meetings to go over new security measures or to answer each other's questions. They even have a chat board set up that many contribute to so they can ask questions and offer advice. So yes, they talk, and they were suspicious of the Awans, as the Awans never contributed to the chat board or came to the meetings.

After the Awans were booted off the House computer network, an IT aide said, "The offices the Awans worked in were trashed. There were no records of the member's computer equipment—this is against House rules—and many of the security protocols weren't up to date. New IT administrators had to start from scratch."

As for Imran Awan's email address being listed as controlling the Apple IDs of these staffer's smartphones, one IT aide said, "There is just no other reason for doing that other than spying. When I set up iPhones for a staffer, I have them use their private email address for their Apple ID. This way they have a privacy wall and, also, if they leave, this gives me a simple way to wipe and reset the phone for another user."

For these reasons and more, security experts say the Awans were actually the definition of insider threats. They were spies. That they were also allegedly running an illegal procurement scheme and perhaps engaging in other types of fraud just gives prosecutors more leverage in their investigation and to potentially get them locked up.

Actually, some attorneys pointed out that this is often the preferred method. If the Department of Justice charges them with spying, then the case takes on a dimension that could involve foreign governments. Because Imran and Hina Alvi are US citizens, they would get public trials in the US court system. This means there would be a discovery process, and perhaps many people would be deposed by defense attorneys. All of that could leak sources, methods, and more used by US intelligence agencies. This could damage future intelligence work, and it could harm relations with other nations, including Pakistan. Now, Pakistan isn't exactly an ally—the United States notably didn't inform Pakistani authorities before sending the Navy SEALs on the raid to get Osama bin Laden. Also, Pakistan, as this was going to print, still had people in jail they've accused of helping the United States find bin Laden—but nevertheless, relations with Pakistan are important in the war on terror.

Authorities in the US State Department would surely advise US attorneys not to press such a case beyond a domestic criminal probe into bank fraud and perhaps other charges. Though that might be a sober view for US intelligence agencies and diplomats to take, it would take the pressure off members of Congress to understand and protect themselves, and therefore our open democratic system, from spies who can embed themselves on a congressional member's staff, especially as an IT administrator who can see all of the emails, sent and received, from a congressional office.

A few members of Congress have noticed how open the House is to spies.

This possibility caused Rep. Steve King (R-IA) to say that the Awans might have funneled information or money "into the hands of the Taliban or ISIS. It could be a coordinated effort to set up a pseudo business here in the House of Representatives for the purposes of gaining access to classified, prioritized information," he said. "Who would that money go to in Pakistan? Family perhaps. But we also know there are extensive and sophisticated money-electing methods in that part of the world."[12]

Could the alleged procurement scam have something to do with espionage?

"The network that's there allowed them to bill for the computer equipment for just a few dollars less than five hundred dollars, then sign a service contract that would be of multiple hours," said Representative King. "They could rake all that money out and move the equipment out because they are not required to inventory computer equipment that's under five hundred dollars. The wages and the computer equipment are not as important, in my view, as access to all of this proprietary information, which may be classified."

King also slammed Rep. Debbie Wasserman Schultz for putting Imran's crew on the congressional payroll and then keeping Imran there even though an investigation exposed that they were spying on and perhaps stealing from Congress.

"It's not a new pattern for her," said King. "She refused to allow the FBI to look at the DNC computers when they wanted to investigate the Russian attempt to hack into the DNC—she hasn't been held adequately accountable for that."

Representative King also noted that "WikiLeaks had emails of Imran and his brothers. If you believe the Russians did the hacking, and they handed the emails over to WikiLeaks, that meant the

Russians had access to a lot of information on Democrat House members. Democrat House members don't want an investigation—they don't want the public to find out what's in the emails, nor do they want Americans to know the facts about how they left their doors wide open to a group that's, at best, scam artists."

Imran's stepmother, Samina Gilani, also gave information that shows Imran behaved as a spy. She is from Pakistan but now lives in Virginia. She doesn't speak English, but she has told the authorities through interpreters that the Awan brothers were paying a Pakistan police officer named Azhar Awan. She says Azhar is their cousin. A search of Facebook showed that a man named "Azhar Awan" works for the Faisalabad police department. Someone by that name was Facebook "friends" with some of Imran's group of former congressional aides.

Court records also show that Imran and Abid Awan had taken money from a man who was later linked to Hezbollah, a militant group based in Lebanon that's considered to be a terrorist organization by the US government.

Even some of Imran's relatives have said he was sending computer equipment to Pakistan. "The relatives said Awan and his brothers were also sending IT equipment, such as iPhones, to the country during the same period in which fraudulent purchase orders for that equipment were allegedly placed in the House, and in which congressional equipment apparently went missing," reported the *Daily Caller*.[13]

Congress should have been prepared for this insider threat. Edward Snowden and Chelsea Manning, whether we think of them as heroes or traitors or some mix of the two, showed the US government what even a low-ranking employee could do if they have access to sensitive or classified files. Those two low-level insiders—Snowden was a federal contractor for Dell working in Hawaii, and Manning was in the US Army with the rank of private first class—were responsible for the biggest leaks US intelligence agencies have experienced in the modern age, yet these congressmen and Capitol Police weren't able to comprehend that the Awans were a threat?

"Snowden has become the buzzword for every kind of security breach. But the Snowden leak was an inside job. The leak was the result of a SharePoint-related issue, not with the SharePoint platform, but with governance decisions (i.e., who has access to what data), monitoring, and oversight," said Steve Marsh, director of product marketing for Metalogix, a company that provides management tools for collaboration platforms. "In Snowden's case, he copied gigabytes of data to thumb drives with little challenge. Snowden was given access to sensitive content that he shouldn't have had access to for the purpose of carrying out his tasks. He was already inside the fortress.

"Somewhere along the line, the security and governance protocols broke down within the NSA, and Snowden was able to access and take sensitive data. The NSA may still not be entirely sure what content was copied. Proactively addressing the insider threat with appropriate security and controls would have made it easier to properly assess the damage. The problem will only grow if government agencies and businesses use the same security and governance protocols as they go to the cloud," said Marsh.[14]

Security experts such as Marsh say government and businesses need to use security tools to encrypt and manage data within a controlled system that limits internal access to sensitive content. First, though, they need to carefully vet the people who have access to this data and to make sure there is adequate oversight of personnel. The human element is usually the weakest link in the security chain. Security experts interviewed for this book all were shocked to hear that after Imran Awan got an IT job in Congress in 2004, he was allowed to bring in his brothers, his friends, and his wife, likely without any of them ever going through a background check.

The House of Representatives is actually uniquely open from a security standpoint because all of its 435 offices are basically run as if they are 435 separate businesses under one roof. This makes it hard to be sure that all of these offices are updating their security protocols and applying new patches to newly discovered threats. As already noted, congressional IT administrators have group meetings and a chat board to try to make certain all the offices are updating their systems to keep them secure. But those are run on a voluntary basis. The Awans were simply allowed to ignore their peers and even House authorities for years by not going to these meetings or participating in the chat board, according to House IT aides.

"You must have a team that not only checks compliance with your security approach but continuously monitors the actions of the hackers and constantly upgrades your approach securing sensitive data," said Dr. Scott Nelson, the CTO and executive vice president at Logic PD, an electronics manufacturer and design-engineering company.

Neither Capitol Police nor the House Office of Inspector General did enough to ensure congressional offices were updating and applying new security protocols. Again, congressmen have always been able to run their offices as if they are separate businesses rather than just offices within Congress. This ties them to their states and, for House members, to their districts. It makes these offices culturally different and more responsive to the individual needs of their constituents. It's a great system that has worked for a long time, but when it comes to IT security in this new digital world, it is madness. All a bad actor has to do is find one office that hasn't updated its security or that has loose hiring standards and they can break into the entire House system.

"The popularity and skyrocketing adoption of cloud-based file sharing and storage services have made it easy for businesses alike to collaborate and share content with multiple users. As businesses turn to cloud storage and sharing platforms such as Google Drive, Dropbox, and others, data leaks become an increasing concern. These services lack the security controls required to mandate and track with whom, how, and when file and content are shared," says Joe Moriarty, cofounder of Content Raven, a cloud-based, content-control and analytics platform. "By adding content controls, protection, tracking, and deep analytics to files, companies can plug security and workflow holes. Content controls enable companies to address security concerns by adding watermarks to files and videos; limits on file viewing, printing, and forwarding; engagement and activity analytics; and more—preventing unauthorized access to data, screenshot taking, credential sharing, and other data leakage risks."

Instead of instituting security layers with checks on the system, such as Moriarty and other experts advocate, congressmen were left to mostly fend for themselves. If they had a good IT administrator and chief of staff, perhaps they had a good security system in place. But congressmen aren't typically IT experts, nor are their chiefs of staff. They are in the political game, not the computer technology field.

Congressmen also typically didn't take the time to secure the devices and data that are physically taken out of congressional buildings on iPhones and other devices.

"Nowadays many companies distribute laptops, tablets, and smartphones enabling employees to work anytime, anyplace. Instead of coming to work to work on fixed desktops, the employee is taking work and company data everywhere (physically). This once secure data leaves the secure company building," said David Arnoux, head of growth at Twoodo, a developer of team collaboration tools.

Imran was even allowed to log in to the House system remotely. This is something congressional IT aides and other staff members can do, and it's important they can, as congressmen and their staffs travel often to their home states and abroad. But Imran was even allowed to log in remotely from Pakistan when he wasn't traveling on official business. Some sources close to the investigation even say Imran worked for months at a time from Pakistan. From a security standpoint, it's maddening that this didn't concern House authorities.

Also, as is often a weakness with any government system, Congress hasn't always been nimble about staying up with the times.

"Organizations implement a security program and think they're done. They're not. Security programs need to continuously adapt in order to meet new threats and environmental changes," said Alan Baker, president and chief consultant at Spitfire Innovations, a consulting firm based in Toronto, Canada. "The security landscape is ever evolving, both on the side of threats and on the side of regulators; organizations need to ensure that their security programs change in response."

These gaping holes in security—all exposed by the Awans—must have been noticed by the Russians, the Chinese, and any savvy foreign intelligence service or corporation that could benefit from spying on congressmen. Many foreign governments and corporations would like to know what congressmen who chair or are on the Appropriations Committee, the Foreign Affairs Committee, the Armed Services Committee, or the Homeland Security Committee are saying.

The emails, texts, internal documents, and more from congressmen in these influential positions could be very valuable to both domestic and foreign entities. The ease with which this group of IT administrators, who are almost all from Pakistan, walked into Congress, likely without even undergoing background checks, must interest foreign intelligence services.

The fact that Imran was copying all the data from "forty or more members of Congress,"[15] according to Rep. Scott Perry (R-PA), at least makes him a potential freelance spy the Russians, Chinese, or whoever could have approached and paid. Remember, one of Imran Awan's relatives said, "For the sake of money they would have done anything."[16]

Still, the *Washington Post* reported that although the FBI's Joint Terrorism Task Force was investigating the Awans, "according to a senior congressional official familiar with the probe, criminal investigators have found no evidence that the IT workers had any connection to a foreign government."[17]

This again is an effort by the mainstream media to say there is nothing to see here, folks, please move on. Which is an embarrassing kind of politics for journalists to play, as payments to a local police official alone could mean there are ties to Pakistani authorities. The Pakistani intelligence agency ISI is known to embed with local police departments, especially in a city as big as Faisalabad.

Also, car dealerships such as Cars International A, which Imran and Abid ran with seed money from a man (Ali al-Attar) linked to Hezbollah who is now wanted by US authorities, are a favorite front for people laundering money or with ties to foreign governments, according to Clare Lopez. Car dealerships provide easy opportunities to launder money and to give owners access to credit reports on Americans. As previously noted, Nasir Khattak, who was the Realtor acting as a middleman between al-Attar and Imran Awan, said in court documents: "It was very bad record-keeping in Cars International... it is close to impossible to make any sense out of all the transactions that happened."[18]

Cars International A certainly had all the signs of being a front. Even the dealership's Facebook page had photos of "staff" members that were clearly taken from other websites. The photo for one "employee" named "James Falls O'Brien," for example, was the same photo used in a hairstyle model catalog.[19]

It's also strange that Cars International A was allowed to borrow vehicles from Khattak's business, located across the street, nor is it clear why Khattak would endanger his existing business to help the Awans. "All of those transactions was to support Cars International A from AAA Motors," Khattak said in his deposition. "That's why I did not make any money from my dealership, because my resources were supporting Cars International A."

Though we don't as yet know if the Awan brothers and the others were involved in international espionage, such as by giving away or selling the congressmen's data they were vacuuming up, it also isn't responsible to say, as the *Washington Post* did, that there is "no evidence that the IT workers had any connection to a foreign government." Other than for political reasons, why would the *Post* make such a claim when a House inspector general report had said the House Democratic Caucus server was "being used for nefarious purposes" by the Awans?

Abid Awan said in his bankruptcy filing he needed to keep ownership of two homes because he was separated from or in the process of getting a divorce from Natalia Soba, a Ukrainian woman. If they were divorcing, as this was being written they appear to have patched things up, as several sources say they are still together. This is interesting because Soba used Abid's residence (7110 Falcon St., Annandale, VA 22003) as her legal address when incorporating her own businesses, which also don't appear to be in business. Soba established Alain LLC in 2009, which BizStanding has listed as "inactive,"[20] Discover EZ Car Buying Co. in 2014, and Regional Car Center Inc. in 2015. Google searches didn't turn up any evidence that these companies are in business.

When suspicious people are opening corporations such as these, companies that don't appear to be designed to make a profit, it should raise concerns with investigating law enforcement that there might be something else going on. Soba, after all, was also on the House payroll as an IT administrator on Imran's crew. She was paid for work in

2010 and 2011 as an IT aide for Reps. Emanuel Cleaver, Ted Deutch, and Gabby Giffords.

Though many in the mainstream media have said that following these facts amounts to a right-wing conspiracy, those same publications meanwhile pressed theories that the Trump campaign colluded with the Russian government based on far less evidence.

As another caveat to all Imran was up to, long after he was ousted from the House system, it was discovered he still had an active secret email account on the House computer system, reported the *Daily Caller*. This secret email address was 123@mail.house.gov. The address was linked to the name of a House staffer, Nathan Bennett, who specializes in intelligence and homeland security matters for Rep. André Carson (D-IN). Court documents show Imran used 123@mail.house.gov in addition to the imran.awan@mail.house.gov account.[21] Bennett has denied knowing about the 123 email address, which shows that, once again, oversight from House authorities was lax and that there was little accountability in the open system.

As this book was being written, Representative Carson was a member of both the House Armed Services Committee and the House Committee on Transportation and Infrastructure. He was also on the subcommittee for Intelligence, Emerging Threats, and Capabilities. Representative Carson's office had previously employed Imran, giving Imran access to all of Carson's emails—emails also copied to a server Imran had control over.

Wouldn't a spy create a secret official email address within the House system? It's hard to say what Imran might have gathered from a congressman who is on the subcommittee for Intelligence, Emerging Threats, and Capabilities, but given Imran's habit of copying data and allegedly stealing House equipment, it's not a leap to wonder if he was at least thinking of selling this information.

Even after being ousted from the House system, Imran did still have a lot of data from Congress; after all, US attorneys gave his lawyer a copy of the hard drive from the House laptop owned by Rep. Debbie Wasserman Schultz that was found in a congressional building after midnight on April 6, 2017. This is the laptop that Wasserman Schultz has desperately tried to keep from law enforcement, for what reason we don't yet know. Whatever this information is, she wants kept out of court, Imran, incredibly, still had access to it as this was being written.

As recounted in chapter 2, the hard-drive copy was included in discovery to Chris Gowen, Imran's attorney, even though at the time the case only involved bank fraud. It's hard to say what the contents of this official laptop might have to do with the bank fraud charges Imran and Hina Alvi were indicted for. Assistant US attorney Michael Marando asked in court to have this data returned. When he did, Gowen looked amused.

Given all this, it's clear that Imran acted as a spy and that he also potentially still has a lot of data from Congress at his disposal. All of this makes it equally clear that Congress is vulnerable and needs to make a lot of changes to tighten up its weaknesses. It isn't clear if Congress is making all of the necessary changes to deal with this new and evolving threat.

This, as you'll see in the next chapter, is also putting American freedom at greater risk.

CHAPTER 7

CONGRESS AND THE SURVEILLANCE STATE

We cannot live in fear of our own intelligence community. They have such power to suck up every bit of every transmission, every communication we ever made. We can't just have them willy-nilly releasing that to the public.

—Senator Rand Paul (R-KY)[1]

Having spies in Congress actually might not be all bad if the spies were more like Edward Snowden or Chelsea Manning. Sure, such a traitorous type is hardly a noble whistleblower, as a whistleblower uses the tools in the Whistleblower Protection Enhancement Act to report fraud, waste, and illegal activity in government—and then the government bureaucracy thanks them for their honesty by destroying their careers. Such is the real-world whistleblower's experience.

Yes, people like Snowden and Manning—who are treated as heroes by many on both sides of the political spectrum—might also release secrets that can harm national security, weaken the US Congress's ability to function, and cause all kinds of mayhem in our political system. But at least we'd know all about it and so could insist government make reforms to protect both the sanctity of government and our rights.

The trouble with Imran Awan and his crew of spies from Pakistan is that members of Congress may have had their emails and more sold to foreign intelligence agencies, which could wreak all kinds of mayhem in our political system, albeit behind the scenes, but the public has been kept in the dark. Without real political consequences for those who allowed the Awans to do all they did, Congress likely won't undergo much-needed reforms.

"There is a lot that's rotten here," says Tom Fitton, president of Judicial Watch, "but it is hard to really get to the bottom of what actually happened because Congress has exempted itself from Freedom of Information Act requests. We can use FOIA to get information from the FBI or the Department of Justice or from the Department of the Interior, for that matter, but not from Congress."

Judicial Watch has made its name by shining a lot of light on wrongdoing in the public sector via FOIA requests and lawsuits designed to force emails, documents, and other information from federal officials into the light. But the organization can't use its favorite tool to force documents out of the offices of our elected representatives in Congress.

"I'm also wondering if Congress—even many Republicans—is ignoring this scandal with the Awans because they don't want other things to come out, such as the names of those who've used a slush fund to hush up staffers who've accused congressmen of sexual harassment," said Finton.[2]

Now, it is fair to argue that, even though Congress exempted itself from public oversight via FOIA requests,[3] it does make public an extensive amount of information about congressional activities through outlets such as the *Congressional Record*, committee reports, hearings, and more. But when it comes to a scandal or another personal issue about members of Congress, such as sexual harassment claims, the public doesn't have the legal right to know who said what.

Because of this, in cases where members aren't interested in investigating other members—since an ethics or other investigation might also harm their special arrangement—nothing happens. This is particularly true when the media doesn't want to pursue a story because it might harm the political party they favor.

Finton argues that one key reason why this is troubling is that our democratic system needs light shined on *all* its various officials and departments, even Congress, to keep them honest and therefore as strong as such institutions can be. A Congress that exempts itself from public scrutiny is a shuffle and a sidestep from being a politburo.

Put another way, why shouldn't Congress be subject to the same information disclosure requirements as the executive branch? The Freedom of Information Act does say that "ensur[ing] an informed citizenry [is] vital to the functioning of a democratic society."

"They simply don't want the light shined on them," says Finton.

To see the real problems inherent in this arrangement—and the consequences of not making politicians face up to what the Awans did and might have done—let's take a look at the system that has shown little interest in publicly addressing this spy case.

During the 138 days or so the US House of Representatives is in session each year, the 435 members of the House and their staffs are crowded into the Cannon, Longworth, and Rayburn House Office Buildings. These low and stately buildings stretch out along Independence Avenue just south of the Capitol Building. They are faced in white marble and limestone and connected by underground tunnels and even a train that whisks members of Congress and their staffers to the Capitol Building and back again.

Entering any of the congressional buildings is as easy as stepping off a sidewalk, pushing a revolving door, and emptying your pockets before passing through a metal detector. If you have a bag, just place it on a little conveyer belt as you would in an airport security line.

Just like that, you'll be walking down crowded halls, passing hardwood doors with little signs beside them listing the names of members of Congress and the states they represent. These signs are no more imposing than the little placards that say "Dentist" or "Attorney at Law" hanging along main streets in Middle America. Step into any of the offices and you'll find yourself in the gaze of a young and friendly staffer sitting at a desk pointed at the door. To your right or left you just might see the congressman at their desk, if he or she is in the office and not in a closed-door meeting.

If you are a constituent of the congressman, walking in and meeting him or her often isn't any harder than meeting a small-town mayor. If they can't or won't meet with you, just hang around outside their office door. If Congress is in session, they'll be in and out and you can follow them down the halls and lob questions at them.

They don't, of course, have to answer your questions, but they really can't completely hide, either. Their favorite escape hatches from journalists amid some scandal or other drama are "member's only" elevators positioned along the corridors. This is an effective dodge, but by simply watching the schedule for votes and committee hearings, it's always possible to find them.

This is how the American system has always functioned. It's a lovely and open arrangement. This big, cumbersome, and still surprisingly open system also allows for real dissent. Different factions of both major political parties now and then break away publicly as they try to refine or steer the party they belong to in a different direction.

Such is why it wasn't surprising that, as most of Congress ignored and refused to investigate the multifaceted spy scandal having to do with Imran Awan, his crew, and the many Democrats who employed them, a small group of Republican congressmen decided to go public with their disproval.

"My fear is, on this case, the ferocity is not where it needs to be," Rep. Ron DeSantis (R-FL) said, with his eyes wandering back to the few reporters who showed for an informal and almost impromptu fact-finding hearing on Capitol Hill on October 10, 2017.

Though the room was almost empty, and only five congressmen would appear, the meeting had the feel of a Freedom Caucus insurgency against the establishment.

Representative DeSantis put his fists together in frustration as he explained that leadership in the House wouldn't push an investigation into the Clinton Foundation, but they nevertheless quickly agreed to investigate the Trump campaign's alleged collusion with Russia. Now he was disturbed that the House wouldn't hold hearings to get answers from the members of Congress who'd employed the Awans.

Right in this chamber was an IT scandal involving spies in Congress, tens of thousands of dollars of stolen equipment, and ghost employees being paid exorbitant salaries, yet House leadership wouldn't even approve an ethics investigation into the members who paid these people chief of staff–level salaries.

Representative DeSantis was worried. The FBI and Capitol Police "could easily make an investigative decision to not just deal with members of Congress and their conduct, and I think that would really be unfortunate," he said. "In terms of the House, at some point you have to stand up for your institution." He then asked rhetorically, with his grammar giving way to his obvious frustration: "Are you just totally feckless, or are you actually wanting to get answers?"[4]

This small fact-finding hearing wasn't sanctioned by Republican leadership in the House or attended by any Democrats. The meeting, which lasted about ninety minutes and, as of July 2018, was the only congressional hearing of any sort held on this matter, was attended by Rep. Louie Gohmert (R-TX), Rep. Jim Jordan (R-OH), Rep. Scott Perry (R-PA), Rep. Ron DeSantis (R-FL), and Rep. Steve King (R-IA). Tom Fitton, president of Judicial Watch, Luke Rosiak, a reporter for the *Daily Caller*, and Patrick Sowers, an IT administrator for members of Congress, were in front of these congressmen to provide what information they could.

"What does Congress need to do to get its act together? We've just ceded so much power," Representative DeSantis asked Finton, adding that Judicial Watch often "gets a lot more answers than Congress."

"In this case [Congress doesn't] have to wait for the Justice Department to figure out what members are up to," said Finton. "You have a House ethics process to help figure that out. You have a House IG process that can help figure that out. You have every tool available to you."

Representative DeSantis was shaking his head with exasperation. He knew Congress has the power to subpoena witnesses, including members of Congress. He was aware that the Constitution gives Congress the power to detain or arrest witnesses, but he also knew Congress hasn't had the political will to use that power for generations.

Today, most publicly held congressional hearings aren't much more than courts of public opinion. Each member on a committee typically gets five minutes to grandstand for C-SPAN until their time is up and a member of the other party gets their five minutes. Back and forth it goes, with any momentum in the questioning of a witness quickly killed when a member from the other party takes their turn.

For these and other reasons, congressional committees often fail to achieve anything. They just ridicule, showboat, applaud, or condemn. To get attention, a congressman needs to come up with a juicy sound bite for cable news. Still, even if they come up with just the right amount of outrage to fuel a witty line, their megaphone is really only as loud as the media's inclination to broadcast it. As a result, scandals like this one involving Democrats often get spun, downplayed, or simply ignored by the disproportionate segment of the media that roots for Democrats.

This hampers the process, because before Congress can summon the political will to hold someone in contempt, it often needs the media to tell the public why an action is warranted. The story needs to be told so the public understands the context and gets mad enough to contact their representatives in Congress to demand answers.

Even when Congress does hold someone in contempt, despite the media apathy for the story, it often doesn't amount to much. Just consider former attorney general Eric Holder's experience. Holder was held in contempt of Congress for clearly obstructing the investigation into Operation Fast and Furious, but he nevertheless wasn't disbarred or punished in any meaningful way because the media treated the case as if it were a congressional witch hunt. Holder would remain attorney general for a while before going on to use his law degree to file lawsuits against the next administration (the Trump administration) on behalf of his new client, the State of California.

Congress also hasn't used its power to arrest and detain a person since 1935. Since then it has referred these contempt cases to the Department of Justice. When the DOJ is run by a different party than the House majority, as was the case when Holder was held in contempt of Congress, it can basically ignore the charge, which is what it did.

The central problem this case exposes, however, isn't that the media can be biased. Actually, the media has been evolving as new cable channels and news organizations have been created in our wide-open digital age to make up for the failings and spin CNN and the *Washington Post* revel in. The big problem here isn't even that Congress is too weak to use the tools it has—historically, it has done a poor job of doing that. The central problem is that so many congressmen refuse to come to terms with the times we are living in, which can expose them to being duped by a group like the Awans or even experts in US intelligence agencies.

"This is going to blow up in the House's face if they don't get ahead of it and start taking it more seriously than they are," Finton said at the unofficial hearing, after noting that congressmen are clearly reluctant to do internal reviews that might censure other members of Congress.

"A proper investigation doesn't seem to be taking place," Representative Perry also said, and then read portions of an internal House IG report into the public record that detailed a lot of what the Awans were up to on the House network and other possible crimes they committed.

Congress Needs to Understand US Intelligence Agencies

If members of Congress can be this easily fooled by IT aides, then they can certainly be led on by tech-savvy people from US intelligence agencies. When the NSA, FBI, and other intelligence agencies come to the Hill, for example, for closed-door sessions with members of Congress and proceed to whisper scary things in members' ears, how many can resist giving up American freedom, a piece at a time, to empower US intelligence agencies if they don't have the expertise to ask the right questions or to see other sides of an issue? Instead, they are more likely to protect their political careers by simply trusting, and not questioning, the power of US intelligence agencies.

The simple explanation for this multifaceted scandal is that the Awans found it was all too easy to fool the more than forty congressmen they worked for. This account has it that in this modern cyber thriller, these members of Congress were simply gullible. Such a tech-savvy person can fool them, goes this point of view, because the average member of Congress really doesn't understand the technology they use—most of us don't.

This is a believable defense—with the exception of those in the congressional offices who wrote off tens of thousands of dollars' worth of iPhones and other equipment—because most congressmen grew up and went to school before we all had smartphones in our pockets and email accounts to check. Members of Congress are typically lawyers, real estate developers, or simply career politicians who rose from state government positions. Background in those fields might give them useful experience with the law and government, but few of them know much about information technology. To them, IT administrators like Imran Awan are tradesmen hired to keep the computers doing their thing. Congressmen could plausibly be fooled by a person with an IT degree from Johns Hopkins, such as Imran Awan has.

It's less plausible that younger staffers would be so easily deceived, but then, IT administrators now working for Congress who were interviewed for this book did say they are rarely watched or questioned. They are, rather, more often treated like tradesmen showing up to get the toilets flushing—and who bothers to really talk to a plumber?

The trouble is, information technology has one big difference from the other trades. An IT administrator, as the story behind what Imran and his crew did shows us, can expose congressmen to all they've said and done online in their conversations with donors, other congressmen, foreign governments, media members, and their voters. This information could be used to shut them up, to destroy their political careers, to make them vote a certain way, or to expose them to corporate or international espionage.

Still, it actually isn't surprising or even terribly important that congressmen are baffled by how the technology they use works. Most congressmen presumably know just as little about graphic design, nursing, or engineering, just as sailors likely know little about shipbuilding. The real problem is that many members of Congress believe our nation's compass, our shared set of values best articulated as the individual liberties specifically protected from government infringement in the Bill of Rights, is no longer a relevant guide in today's digital age. As a result, they are sailing us into new and dangerous seas without knowing, or thinking it important to know, the difference between north and south.

This makes them particularly susceptible in this digital age to being led away from American constitutional values by personnel in US intelligence agencies who, though they likely have commendable intentions, want to empower their agencies by weakening long-held principles of American privacy and freedom. US intelligence experts, after all, can easily baffle members of Congress (and most of us) with technological terms and scare them with new threats from abroad that are classified and so kept from being balanced via public discussion.

The founders addressed this problem in a fundamental, if bookish, way. They required members of Congress to take an oath of office. The oath was mandated in the Constitution, but the wording of it was left to the first Congress to write. Congress has altered it several times over the centuries. Today's oath, however, hasn't changed in half a century (since 1966). It is set down in Title 5, Section 3331 of the US Code. It reads: "I, AB, do solemnly swear (or affirm) that I will support and defend the Constitution of the United States against all enemies, foreign and domestic; that I will bear true faith and allegiance to the same; that I take this obligation freely, without any mental reservation or purpose of evasion, and that I will well and faithfully discharge the duties of the office on which I am about to enter. So help me God."[5]

This oath was meant to help congressmen navigate us toward liberty and freedom even as they legislate in new and complex areas that might be outside their expertise. In this way, in any debate or crisis, all they have to do is look back to the US Constitution and its twenty-seven amendments to regain sure footing. If they don't do this, the courts or the executive branch are supposed to check them, again by looking back to our founding document. After the Patriot Act passed with a bipartisan vote without much debate, amid intense fear after the 9/11 terrorist attacks, it was found that many parts of the act trampled on First and Fourth Amendment restrictions. A series of court decisions in the ensuing years, and political pressure on Congress, did strike down many of the most egregious oversteps, which had had been supported by US intelligence agencies.

There is also a constitutional process for dealing with these oversteps by government. If the public is unhappy enough with where our founding document is leading us, then they can push to amend the Constitution, which has happened many times throughout American history. That clear constitutional process has long kept, or tried to keep, the republic on a sound course. (Anyone who tells you the Constitution is a "living document," say to them, "Yes it is. We can amend it.")

From this constitutional bearing, members of Congress and their staffs should have seen Imran Awan and his crew as the insider threats to their careers and to the integrity of the system they were. The Fourth Amendment's "right of the people to be secure in their persons, houses, papers, and effects, against unreasonable searches and seizures" includes congressmen. This should have made them think about securing their data and our data as they upheld their oaths.

Even their selfish self-interest to keep their jobs should have told them to be careful of insider threats who can use their own emails against them. Might the fact that this is a sore issue with Democrats after their 2016 loss explain why so many Democrats have adamantly stuck to the narrative that it was the Russians who hacked the DNC and not, possibly, an insider who actually released the data? Could this view also have blinded them to an insider threat like the Awans?

Instead of using the Constitution or even common sense as a guide, the Democrats who hired the Awans chose political correctness. They turned a blind eye to what Imran and his crew might do and likely did do for years, since they viewed the Awans as part of a protected group of immigrants.

Congress has been such a ship of fools on these issues that when a congressional committee called politically appointed bureaucrats from the IRS, such as Lois Lerner, then director of the Exempt Organizations unit of the IRS (she was previously general counsel for the Federal Election Commission), before them to explain a scandal in which IRS employees had used their regulatory authority to silence groups with certain politics before the 2012 presidential election, the bureaucrats simply pleaded the Fifth, shrugged, and behaved as if they were in a kangaroo court, because they basically were.

If Republican congressmen—or Democrats, for that matter—had pointed out that this IRS scandal was about First Amendment–protected free speech instead of allowing the narrative to be taken over and muddled in the media, they'd have gotten more traction. First Amendment–protected speech, after all, is one of the few issues that almost everyone, from progressives to conservatives, agrees is important. Taking a stand for free speech is the moral and American thing to do. But though some did this, Republican leadership never understood this enough to get everyone on the same clear message and articulate it to the American people and thereby shove this honest message right through the media filter.

That's the turbulent political sea Congress foolishly sailed us into, pushed on by progressive winds from the mainstream media, but let's get to the concrete things that can right the ship. To clearly expose the broader implications of this problem, let's use the Constitution as a guide to areas that have recently affected American security and freedom, such as the Awans exploited.

Shouldn't the Constitution Protect Us at the Border?

While doing research for this book I had many off-the-record conversations with men and women from US intelligence agencies. I also interviewed people who work for Congress and others who want their names kept out of print. None of these individuals told me about secret government programs or anything that would make an interesting plot for the next Jason Bourne movie. What I mostly got was background and perspective—invaluable things to a journalist who wants to get things right. But recordings of some of those conversations are on my iPhone. Contact information for other sources is there, too. So I've password-protected the encrypted data. and my iPhone will automatically erase all the texts, audio, and more if someone tries to hack their way into it via a "dictionary attack."

That's my reason for being concerned that US Customs and Border Protection has the power to disregard my Fourth Amendment rights and demand I give them access to my digital devices if I fly internationally or even decide to drive to Montreal.

I'm a journalist and I must protect my sources, but I also don't think my private photos, my social media, my texts, and my contacts are the government's business—at least without a warrant from a US court. Yes, I have a healthy American distrust of authority.

Of course, like any sane person, I also want the US government to nab terrorists before they shoot any of us or blow us to pieces.

Therein lies a dilemma of our time. Should we give up privacy for *perceived* security? I say "perceived" because the more I look into issues related to this question, the less I am inclined to believe it makes us safer to let the government have loopholes right through the Fourth Amendment's protections of our "persons, houses, papers and effects against unreasonable searches and seizures."

Actually, giving them this kind of power can flood our intelligence agencies with so much data that the real bad guys' data becomes a needle in the haystack. Such a data flood also takes precious resources away from the solid police work our law enforcement and intelligence agencies really need to be doing (and often do so well).

There are many other dangers inherent in empowering government in this way, but let's focus on this growing loophole that allows US Customs and Border Protection, without a warrant, to gain access to what has become a vast depository of our most private photos, thoughts, contacts, and associations—yes, our smartphones and laptops.

Sure, anyone who travels knows we give up a lot when we fly. We literally surrender as we put up our hands inside booths that scan our bodies. We take out our laptops and put them on conveyer belts. We take off our shoes and shuffle along in our socks. We sit in seats that now average just 17 inches wide, down from 18.5 inches in the early 2000s, according to a lawsuit filed by Flyers Rights. All along we know our bags can be searched at any time. And we know this is done to enhance our safety, so we comply; in fact, we'd alert the authorities if we saw something suspicious.

But should this mean that when we travel internationally, CBP should be able to search our smartphones and laptops without a warrant?

The courts have given the government a lot of power to search at the border. In *United States v. Flores-Montano* (2004), the Supreme Court ruled "[t]he Government's interest in preventing the entry of unwanted persons and effects is at its zenith at the international border." Back in 1977, in *United States v. Ramsey*, the Court established "[t]hat searches made at the border, pursuant to the long-standing right of the sovereign to protect itself by stopping and examining persons and property crossing into this country, are reasonable simply by virtue of the fact that they occur at the border." For our safety, said the Court in *United States v. Montoya de Hernandez* in 1985, "[r]outine searches of the persons and effects of entrants are not subject to any requirement of reasonable suspicion, probable cause, or warrant."

Most of those precedents predate smartphones. We used to just have photos of our kids in our wallets. Now we now walk around with digital libraries of our personal lives. To invade those spaces, clearly the U.S government must be required to obtain a warrant based on probable cause.

After all, even at the border the Fourth Amendment doesn't become invisible ink; legally speaking, it's just that routine searches become reasonable because the government needs to find bombs or illegal goods. So yes, we can all appreciate that CBP agents need to search bags and scan electronic devices for guns, bombs, and more. But now these searches of our electronic devices are becoming common. On April 11, 2017, the CBP announced in a press release it had searched 14,993 electronic devices being carried by international travelers (the agency didn't say how many were American citizens). In all of 2016, CBP says it searched 19,033 devices. In 2015, reports say it searched about 5,000.

Some searches of journalists have even made headlines. In October 2016, CBP agents denied a Canadian photojournalist, Ed Ou, entry into the United States after he refused to give them access to the data on his phones.

In July 2016, CBP agents detained a *Wall Street Journal* reporter, Maria Abi-Habib, who is an American citizen, and asked for access to her cell phones. She refused. The agents eventually released her without seizing or searching her devices.

Maria Abi-Habib wrote a Facebook post on the event in which she said in part:

> [A CBP agent] handed me a DHS document, a photo of which I've attached. It basically says the US government has the right to seize my phones and my rights as a US citizen (or citizen of the world) go out the window. This law applies at any point of entry into the US, whether naval, air or land and extends for 100 miles into the US from the border or formal points of entry. So, all of NY city for instance. If they forgot to ask you at JFK airport for your phones, but you're having a drink in Manhattan the next day, you technically fall under this authority. And because they are acting under the pretense to protect the US from terrorism, you have to give it up.
>
> So I called their bluff.
>
> "You'll have to call The Wall Street Journal's lawyers, as those phones are the property of WSJ," I told her, calmly.
>
> She accused me of hindering the investigation—a dangerous accusation as at that point, they can use force. I put my hands up and said I'd done nothing but be cooperative, but when it comes to my phones, she would have to call WSJ's lawyers.[6]

It's important to also consider the government's side, as it is trying to protect us. Governments have, after all, had spies pose as journalists. In the United States it's especially easy to do so, since in the age of social media we are *all* the media. There are no official media credentials, and there shouldn't be—freedom would go away pretty fast if the government got to decide who is officially a member of the media.

Also, many of the searches of journalists' digital devices that have made the biggest waves have tended to be of people who have traveled to countries with known terror links.

The CBP argued: "The increase of electronic device searches is driven by CBP's mission to protect the American people and enforce the nation's laws in this digital age. CBP has adapted and adjusted its actions to align with current threat information. CBP border searches of electronic devices have resulted in evidence helpful in combating terrorist activity, child pornography, violations of export controls, intellectual property rights violations, and visa fraud."[7]

So what's the right balance?

"They should have to comply with the Fourth Amendment's protections," says Adam Schwartz, senior staff attorney for the Electronic Frontier Foundation. "We have submitted amicus briefs in several cases in hopes that the Supreme Court will require the government to get a warrant before invading the privacy of US citizens."[8]

Schwartz also notes this is a question the Supreme Court hasn't specifically answered in the modern era—after digital devices grew into things that can contain so much of our private lives.

If the US government has a person on a watch list, sees reason to search based on probable cause, and so on, then it should be able to detain the person and go to a judge to obtain a warrant to search their digital devices. Outside of that scenario, allowing government agents to simply access a US citizen's contacts, social media, videos, and everything else in search of a crime doesn't feel American, because it isn't.

This is actually the type of warrantless, invasive search the Fourth Amendment was included in our Bill of Rights to prevent. When legislating on this issue, Congress should just apply our Fourth Amendment-protected rights to this situation. If CBP or the FBI advises Congress that it needs this power to nab incoming ISIS fighters—and presents evidence in a closed-door hearing to prove the point—fine. Congress should respect that agency's hard work and point of view by pointing out this constitutional restriction on government only protects US citizens. When dealing with them, the agency must get a warrant.

Should the Government Be Able to Do Backdoor Searches?

In 2017, the explanations from the US intelligence agencies about how they use the FISA Amendments Act began to sound like Leslie Nielsen did in *The Naked Gun* films when he stood in front of exploding mayhem shouting, "Nothing to see here, folks. Please disburse."

The FISA Amendments Act is a 2008 law that allows the National Security Agency to tap the communications of "non-US persons" who are outside the United States but also allows the NSA to sidestep the Fourth Amendment protections of US citizens by recording their emails and phone calls if they happen to communicate with people overseas.

This was stalled in Congress as different interest groups pushed back against such warrantless surveillance, but then Republican leadership in the House of Representatives suddenly pushed the measure through on a vote of 256–164. At the behest of US intelligence agencies, Republicans and some Democrats renewed the controversial Section 702 of the Foreign Intelligence Surveillance Act (FISA). This section of the act allows US intelligence agencies to listen in on phone calls, read emails, and more of non-US citizens. It's controversial because the NSA and other agencies also listen in on an unknown number of communications from American citizens—something the Fourth Amendment was written to keep the government from doing unless it first obtains a warrant from a court.

President Donald J. Trump first posted on Twitter: "This is the act that may have been used, with the help of the discredited and phony Dossier, to so badly surveil and abuse the Trump Campaign by the previous administration and others?"

But then someone got in the president's ear, as Trump soon clarified his position by tweeting: "With that being said, I have personally directed the fix to the unmasking process since taking office and today's vote is about foreign surveillance of foreign bad guys on foreign land. We need it! Get smart!"

Many Democrats and some Republicans wanted to amend the act to prevent the government from stepping right over the Fourth Amendment—45 Republicans and 119 Democrats voted against the renewal of this legislation.

"In light of the significant concerns that have been raised by members of our caucus, and in light of the irresponsible and inherently contradictory messages coming out of the White House today, I would recommend that we withdraw consideration of the bill today, to give us more time to address the privacy questions that have been raised, as well as to get a clear statement from the administration about their position on the bill," said Rep. Adam Schiff (D-CA), who is the top Democrat on the House Permanent Select Committee on Intelligence.

Before approving a six-year extension of the law, the House voted 233–183 to kill an amendment designed to protect Americans' civil liberties. This amendment, proposed by Rep. Justin Amash (R-MI), would have required officials to get warrants in most cases before intercepting and reading the electronic communications of US citizens.

This legislation was contentious even in Congress after members found out they had skin in the game. Recent "unmaskings" showed them that even a congressman's conversations with a foreign official might go public with their names un-redacted. This way, even if the member of Congress didn't do anything wrong, what they said and whom they spoke with could quickly be taken out of context by the media outlets that root for the opposing team.

To make this point clear, Republicans even used a debate at a congressional hearing in 2017 to suggest Obama administration officials purposely unmasked elected officials and then leaked the info to harm Trump administration officials. Specifically, former national security advisor Susan Rice and former US ambassador to the United Nations Samantha Power were accused of unmasking Trump administration officials and expanding who could see the documents in an effort to get them to leak.

This is why Sen. Rand Paul (R-KY) said, "We cannot live in fear of our own intelligence community. They have such power to suck up every bit of every transmission, every communication we ever made. We can't just have them willy-nilly releasing that to the public."

Now the NSA can continue to ignore our Fourth Amendment.

Perhaps you are wondering how many Americans our government is listening in on? Sorry, we don't know. The intelligence agencies told Congress they couldn't say just how many American citizens have been eavesdropped on by the government (without warrants).

Correcting this problem begins with pushing a change in mindset. Too often our intelligence agencies, as law enforcement will, have their eyes so fixed on the problems—terrorism, online crime syndicates, ransomware wielded by criminal gangs—they lose sight of the freedom they are supposed to be protecting. People in the US government have too often decided that part of their mission is to weaken American freedom to empower themselves. The federal government even outlawed computer encryption until the courts forced it to get out of the way in the early 1990s—this happened after computer source code for encryption was printed in a book to give it clear First Amendment protections.

Bridging this divide actually isn't that hard—the American constitutional system is built to rectify these kinds of privacy-versus-security debates.

US intelligence agencies should simply be required to abide by Fourth Amendment protections. Congress, after all, could set up a legal apparatus to help to quickly give the NSA and other agencies the ability to get approval or, in some cases, to get approval within a certain time period after the fact for listening in on communications that might include US citizens. Yes, this means stripping away the NSA's ability to listen away with no checks or balances from Congress or the courts. Fourth Amendment protections need to be respected. If technology makes it possible for the NSA to listen in on conversations, then the NSA, with all of its vast resources, can propose ways for technology to help create a fast approval and oversight process.

Meanwhile, civil libertarians shouldn't forget that US intelligence agencies have an almost impossible task. They have to find terrorists and others who are plotting to do us harm in an age when encryption and other technologies allow even unsophisticated criminals to hide their communications. But then, history is also a teacher here—there is no secret to what happens when government organizations are allowed to secretly trample on their citizens' rights.

Should the Government Be Able to Take Away Online Anonymity?

In a 2017 case that cracked the foundation of online freedom, Judge Diane J. Humetewa of the US District Court for the District of Arizona ruled that the US Department of Justice could force a private company—say, Facebook, Yelp, or Twitter—to give up your identity simply because you expressed an opinion online.

This ruling occurred after the DOJ obtained a grand jury subpoena to make Glassdoor, an online job-review website, give up the identities of eight people (the DOJ initially wanted the identities of 125 people). The DOJ wants their internet protocol addresses, their credit card information, and other identifying details so it can find these eight people, question them, and perhaps compel them to testify against a company the DOJ is investigating.

So although Glassdoor proudly says it has "succeeded in protecting the anonymity of our members in more than eighty cases" via civil suits filed by companies that are ticked off about something someone posted anonymously, this is a criminal case related to an unknown private company.

Now, any reasonable person likely understands why federal prosecutors want to speak to these witnesses, but forcing a private company to give up people's personal information would set a precedent that would allow Big Brother–style intrusions anytime the government wants to know who said what.

Glassdoor tried to avoid this constitutional fight by offering to instead post a notice on its site asking people to come forward to give information. Glassdoor has done that before. But that wasn't enough for the DOJ.

To parry this attempt to unmask private citizens, Glassdoor, a California-based company, appealed the ruling to the Ninth Circuit Court of Appeals.

This has made it a clear constitutional fight. If this ruling stands, then any comment you make on Facebook, Twitter, or Yelp could give the federal government the power to find out your real identity—even if you aren't accused of committing a crime. Your personal information might then go public, as it could be available via a Freedom of Information Action request or other means to your employer and anyone else. In such an environment, would members of a labor union pause before freely expressing their views to one another? Would whistleblowers decide not to give information "anonymously" because they might be exposed?

"We'd like a precedent set that respects American freedom in today's world," said Brad Serwin, general counsel at Glassdoor. "The government is arguing they should be able to find out someone's identity as long as it is not acting in 'bad faith.' We're arguing that, legally speaking, the government is required to pass a 'compelling interest' test before being given the authority to demand people's identities from a private company. We believe the lower court applied the wrong standard in placing the interests of government ahead of Americans' protected free speech rights under the First Amendment. We hope to persuade the US Ninth Circuit Court of Appeals to require a higher standard for these requests."[9]

Fourth Amendment protections don't necessarily block this, because the government is going after a private company (a third party) for these people's info, so according to the Supreme Court's "third-party doctrine," these people have "no reasonable expectation of privacy." So yeah, according to this judge, all those pseudonyms we see on social media and in comment sections below articles are no protection from snooping Big Brother if the government wants to know who is speaking anonymously.

Whatever the outcome of the appeal to the Ninth Circuit, the Supreme Court should weigh in eventually, since the legal precedents being cited in this case are old (before the internet age) and unclear. Glassdoor argues the Ninth Circuit should apply a "compelling/substantial connection test" from *Bursey v. United States*, a 1972 decision that involved members of the Black Panthers who were held in contempt after they refused to answer questions from a federal grand jury. The government, meanwhile, thinks the test in *Branzburg v. Hayes*, a 1972 Supreme Court case that invalidated the use of the First Amendment as a defense for reporters summoned to testify before a grand jury, should be used.

Outside of the constitutionally protected rights being affected here, there is a more practical reason for Glassdoor—and for any website that allows online reviews or comments—to fight such a ruling: it undermines their business model. Glassdoor allows individuals to post incognito reviews of employers, which gives other people information about an employer they might be considering a job offer from. Glassdoor says it gets about forty-five million unique visitors every month. But how many people would post a critical review of a current or former employer if they thought the government might reveal their identity, not because of any criminal fault of their own, but because the government says it has an interest compelling it to force them into the public light?

Maybe this Arizona judge is simply an outlier, as other judges have ruled differently on similar cases. In *SunEnergy1, LLC, et al. v. Jeffrey Lawrence Brown*, for example, the court ruled: "The content of the reviews on Glassdoor.com are such that it should be obvious to any reasonable person that the authors (all listed as current or former employees) are using the website as a vehicle to express their personal opinions about the company in question. Glassdoor.com is a website for employment and company evaluation—it is not a news website (e.g. WSJ.com or NYT.com) where there is an expectation of objective reporting and journalistic standards."

This is clearly one of those cases where Congress shouldn't be afraid to check the executive branch, as the DOJ is arguing it should be able to attain this personal data without a warrant. It doesn't take a deep understanding of computer information systems to understand what Congress's role is here. As the members' oath says, they should protect the Constitution. In this case, that means protecting the Fourth Amendment. US citizens, after all, should not have to fear their federal government will compel disclosure of their identities without their consent when they have committed no crime.

Should the Government Be Allowed to Find Out Who Opposes It Politically?

In 2017, a Washington, DC, court ordered DreamHost to give the Department of Justice data on some anti-Trump protesters. Federal prosecutors were trying to identify and charge activists who'd acted violently. But to find them, the DOJ demanded that DreamHost, a web-hosting provider and domain-name registrar, give up data that could identify the million-plus people who'd used the political-organizing website #Disruptj20.org.

The DOJ argued in a motion to the court that "the website disruptj20.org was used to organize a riot that took place in the District of Columbia on the morning of January 20, 2017.... The Warrant is focused on evidence of the planning, coordination and participation in a criminal act—that is, a premeditated riot. The First Amendment does not protect violent, criminal conduct such as this."[10]

Nevertheless, this case quickly became the front lines for internet freedom, as the government was seeking much more than the specific information about those who acted criminally. The court ultimately narrowed the scope of the warrant.

Had DreamHost complied without a fight or lost, internet anonymity (via the Fourth Amendment restriction that forces government to get a warrant before searching our "persons, houses, papers, and effects") would have been weakened yet again. If the government had gotten its way, then federal authorities, by using any person's alleged crime as a rationale, could have demanded a broad range of personal records on Americans from private companies in order to mine data for crimes or other purposes.

If the Fourth Amendment protects anything, it prevents the government from going wherever it pleases to simply search for crimes.

After the court hearing, DreamHost declared a partial victory: "We've got great news for internet users around the world today: We did it. We made the internet better."[11]

DreamHost said, "Our argument was straightforward—information that could be used to identify tens of thousands of internet users who simply visited the website would have been handed over to the US government in a sweeping request for data. In our opinion, this was a clear case of investigatory overreach."

If the government had gotten all it wanted, then any journalist who'd visited #Disruptj20.org could have ended up on a government list, as could any citizen.

The DOJ's response to this worry was essentially: trust us, we won't create a political dissidents' list:

> The Warrant—like the criminal investigation—is singularly focused on criminal activity. It will not be used for any other purpose. Contrary to DreamHost's claims, the Warrant was not intended to be used, and will not be used, to "identify the political dissidents of the current administration[.]" Nor will it be used to "chill [ ] free association and the right of free speech afforded by the Constitution." In fact, as discussed further below, after conducting a careful search and seizing the evidence within the scope of the Warrant, law enforcement will set aside any information that was produced by DreamHost but is outside the scope of the Warrant; it will seal that information; and it will not revisit that information without a further court order.[12]

Given how government power has recently been used for political purposes (see the IRS's treatment of conservative nonprofits before the 2012 election, the DOJ's use of wiretaps on journalists during the Obama administration, and the alleged "unmaskings" of officials for political purposes), it requires more than a little naivety to simply trust government with data of those who likely oppose the current administration.

Still, given emerging technology, the legal precedent here is even more important.

Citing a previous ruling, the DOJ argued the "federal courts are in agreement that a warrant authorizing the seizure of a defendant's home computer equipment and digital media for a subsequent off-site electronic search is not unreasonable or overbroad, as long as the probable cause showing in the warrant application and affidavit demonstrate a 'sufficient chance of finding some needles in the computer haystack.'"

Yes, but this wasn't "a defendant's home computer." That phrasing implies that a specific warrant would be used to search the devices of a single residence or person. This instead was a broad demand for data from a web-hosting company that would have effectively been a blanket warrant to search over a million people's data simply because they had visited a website.

For this reason, the court narrowed the data DreamHost had to hand over and said it will offer oversight to ensure the data is not used for any other purpose than prosecuting those who damaged property or hurt people.

What this case shows is technology doesn't mean, by default, that we must lose our Fourth Amendment protections. To keep our privacy, we must demand that our constitutional protections are applied to current and new technologies. Technology can preserve privacy or it can take it away. There is actually a fundamental war going on between private companies, like Apple, that create technology the government can't crack and the intelligence agencies that attempt to weaken, crack, or infiltrate this technology. The war hasn't been won or lost by either side but is ongoing. Our freedom hangs in the balance, as does our security.

Again, this is an area where Congress should step in to check the courts or the executive branch by writing and passing legislation that protects Fourth Amendment rights in this modern digital environment. To do so, it simply must use the Bill of Rights as its compass to navigate these new digital seas.

Freedom Is in the Balance

There is no shortage of other examples where, in the digital age, Congress needs to find its constitutional bearings and protect US citizens from government overreach as it works with Capitol Police, the FBI, the NSA, and others to enhance domestic and national security.

The Awans, after all, were insider threats Congress failed to see or understand. This also can impact American freedom. If a congressman's emails or other data are stolen by insiders or hackers, that information might be used to game the political system, blackmail a congressman, predict how legislation might affect stock prices, or do countless other criminal things and/or acts of espionage that could impact any person or industry in the United States.

This makes Plato's "ship of fools" allegory particularly relevant with regard to today's Congress. Like the sailors in Plato's story, congressmen are in an endless argument as they try to navigate new waters they don't comprehend. Their political clamor and ignorance with regard to changes in technology often makes them agree too easily with experts in computer technology, law enforcement, and intelligence who tell them freedom must be weakened to enhance security. These experts' opinions are often valuable, but they need to be tempered by the men and women who are elected to ensure that such recommendations fit into our constitutional framework, a system fine-tuned to keep us free and as safe as possible in this evolving world.

Technology must also be used to safeguard our freedom. We must demand and force the intelligence community to simply defend the walls of our freedom instead of requiring us to give up our freedom in the name of saving it. If, in the wake of cases like the Awans, we fall for the false narrative that we must give up privacy for perceived security, then we'll lose everything in the name of preserving the American way of life.

CHAPTER 8

COVER UP

Today is the beginning of a new day for Imran, which we, his lawyers, along with so many of his friends and family, sincerely celebrate. We cannot be as optimistic about the political and media culture that had no problem destroying Imran's life, but we urge that this deep injustice of Imran's case be taken as a wake-up call on a worsening situation.

—Chris Gowen, Imran Awan's attorney

Anyone who reads the FBI affidavit[1] used to indict Imran Awan can plainly see even a prosecutor working on their first case wouldn't have had any trouble getting a conviction for bank fraud (see, Chapter 3). Yet, the Department of Justice opted to plea the crimes down to one count of making one false statement on a home equity loan application. In return, all the DOJ got was something less than they already had.

On July 3, 2018, in return for pleading guilty to just one count of making one false statement, the DOJ gave Imran Awan and Hina Alvi a sweetheart plea-deal agreement. Hina Alvi would have all charges against her dismissed. As for Imran, this plea-deal agreement stipulated he "will not be charged" for any other nonviolent crime he had already disclosed to the DOJ—just what he disclosed the DOJ won't say.

So just like that, the DOJ tried to make this case go away.

The plea-deal agreement even attempted to exonerate Imran by saying in part that "the Government agrees that the public allegations that your client [Imran Awan] stole U.S. House of Representatives ('House') equipment and engaged in unauthorized or illegal conduct involving House computer systems do not form the basis of any conduct relevant to the determination of the sentence in this case...."

It's true that evidence of other crimes clearly aren't relevant to the bank fraud indictment. Those charges were simple. Imran had been caught lying in order to fraudulently get his hands on a lot of runaway money. But those other facts had a lot to do with other crimes that may have been committed.

"Particularly," also says the plea-deal agreement, "the Government has found no evidence that your client [Imran Awan] illegally removed House data from the House network or from House Members' offices, stole the House Democratic Caucus Server, stole or destroyed House information technology equipment, or improperly accessed or transferred government information, including classified or sensitive information."

This is an odd claim, especially given that the DOJ gives no evidence to back it up.

Some of the missing House devices were found in a garage by a tenant of Imran's (see, Chapter 4). Another $120,000 worth of equipment had been written off from Rep. Yvette Clarke's (D-NY) office (see, Chapter 1). Now, some sources say this $120,000 has more to do with Imran's brother Abid, but so what? File charges against Abid and investigate. The money trail won't be hard to follow. Prosecutors easily had enough information from congressional paperwork alone to get House staffers to talk.

As for the "improperly accessed or transferred government information, including classified or sensitive information," there is a lot of forensic evidence showing that the Awans were copying congressmen's data to the House Democratic Caucus server and even to a private Dropbox account. Imran and his crew were even tossed off the House system because they provided false information (a fake copy of the Democratic Caucus' server) to Capitol Police.

I sat flabbergasted as the plea-deal was explained in court.

When I asked the DOJ prosecutor who appeared in court to make this deal public, J.P. Cooney, why the government made this odd deal when they clearly had Imran cold on the bank fraud charge, and when they didn't get anything else in return (at least nothing they've made public), he just smiled and waved me away, as if it was all a big joke, as he told me to ask the DOJ's public affairs department. The DOJ's public affairs department did issue a press release, but they declined to answer any further questions.

Again, they were simply moving to make this all go away.

The court scene didn't just smell like a cover up by the establishment, it reeked of corruption in Congress and the DOJ. This is clearly a political deal arranged to protect the establishment from further embarrassment and reform.

Real court scenes (when he pleaded guilty, Imran Awan waved his right to a trial by jury), possible depositions of House staffers and members of Congress, and the investigations that would take place if the DOJ did pursue additional charges would have necessarily dug into a lot of things the Washington establishment would rather not deal with publicly. It also would have forced investigators to follow the trail to Pakistan—something the US intelligence community would rather avoid.

Still, I didn't think these investigating agencies would be brazen enough to agree to this kind of a sweetheart deal for Imran Awan and Hina Alvi.

The deal also gave the many mainstream media members who'd downplayed and ignored this case (a few sources told me they'd brought detailed information to the *Washington Post*, but that the *Post* ignored the information) cover and a reason to thumb their noses at the few media members who'd done serious work on this case.

"This case illustrates the real and tragic human consequences of a right-wing media operation that today goes far beyond mere political opportunism. For the past 19 months my client, Imran Awan has been the target of a coordinated effort by House Republicans, the President, and right-wing 'media' in an effort to destroy the reputation of a dedicated public servant for political purposes. Today's plea deal resolves, in black and white, that all of the coordinated allegations were not true. My client is not a 'spy,' nor part of a 'spy ring.' There has never been any missing server, smashed hard drives, blackmailed members of Congress, or breach of classified information. This was all made up, for purposes of clickbait, Fox News stories, and political opportunism," said Chris Gowen, Imran's attorney, in a statement after the plea-deal hearing.

The *Washington Post* was smug. After the plea-deal hearing they ran a story under the headline "Ex-congressional IT staffer reaches plea deal that debunks conspiracy theories about illegal information access."

> Federal prosecutors concluded an 18-month investigation into a former congressional technology staffer on Tuesday by publicly debunking allegations—promoted by conservative media and President Trump—suggesting he was a Pakistani operative who stole government secrets with cover from House Democrats.
>
> As part of an agreement with prosecutors, Imran Awan pleaded guilty to a relatively minor offense unrelated to his work on Capitol Hill: making a false statement on a bank loan application. U.S. prosecutors said they would not recommend jail time.
>
> But the agreement included an unusual passage that described the scope of the investigation and cleared Awan of a litany of conspiracy theories promulgated on Internet blogs, picked up by right-leaning news sites and fanned by Trump on Twitter.

The *Washington Post* was once the newspaper of Watergate investigation fame. Every wannabe journalist watches the 1976 film "All the President's Men" and dreams of being Dustin Hoffman (Carl Bernstein) or Robert Redford (Bob Woodward). But that case had to do with the crimes of a Republican president and administration. When it comes to Democrats, the *Post* ignores what journalistic ethics it has. They didn't look into this case, and did all they could to protect the Democrats who'd employed Imran and his crew.

Still, though the mainstream media might have enabled this cover up to be as brazen as it is, the cover up of this case is the result of the establishment in Congress and the DOJ protecting itself. All of the Republicans who refused to talk about or to insist on a real investigation into what was allowed to happen in Congress in this case should ask themselves if Democrats would have helped them cover up if 44 House Republicans had hired, overpaid, given free rein to, and protected a group like the Awans.

Rep. Chris Stewart (R-Utah) did sit down with me to answer questions about this case. Stewart is on the House Permanent Select Committee on Intelligence. He is also on the CIA Subcommittee. He explained that he didn't think this case was such a big deal. "Also," he said, "there are so many other things we have to investigate."

I told him I didn't find his point of view surprising given that when this case broke, only the staffers of the members of Congress who'd employed Imran and his crew were initially briefed. Given that they were all Democrats, they were able to do damage control before the information started to leak out. Also, given the mainstream media's apathy for going after Democrats, it isn't shocking that Republicans, even though they controlled Congress during this time, haven't felt real media pressure to look into this or even to have an ethics investigation into why Rep. Debbie Wasserman Schultz's (D-FL) kept paying Imran even after he was tossed off the House system for providing false information to Capitol Police.

When I began to give Stewart more facts on the case, he did look surprised. He simply didn't know the details. Like Stewart, many Republicans were likely too busy with other investigations and legislation to grasp the importance of this internal investigation.

Still, a lot of noise was raised by a few Republican members of Congress. This should have woken up the leadership. Instead, they chose to ignore this case and to just trust that security protocols would be tightened in Congress.

Stewart even said, "The only reason I am talking to you about this is because I have nothing to give you."

Stewart was willing to go on the record. Many other members of Congress were not. In fact, Speaker of the House Paul Ryan (R-Wis.) and others in the Republican leadership declined to even talk about this case.

Meanwhile, Democrats did all they could to avoid talking about the Awans. When confronted publicly, they'd either quickly walk away or would accuse a reporter asking real questions of pushing conspiracy theories or even of being a racist Islamophobe.

It is unclear how this deal was struck inside the DOJ. Cooney, who showed up to manage the plea-deal hearing, had just been put on this case a few days before. The previous DOJ attorney, Michael Marando, wasn't even in the courtroom.

Clearly, the establishment moved to protect itself. The Democrats who'd employed Imran and his associates weren't cooperating, as news of what the Awans did could harm them politically. But that wouldn't or shouldn't stop an investigation. In this case, the establishment of both parties had a lot to lose if real investigations took place, charges were filed, and Imran and perhaps others on his team were taken to court.

Doing so would have shined a light on how members of Congress hire and pay staffers and on their budgets. Other information, such as which members had used a slush fund to hush up alleged sexual-harassment claims, might then go public. Many congressmen would rather not have public attention, thanks to complex charges filed against House IT contractors that focused in on the special deals and excesses of the political swamp.

If President Donald J. Trump really does want to drain the swamp—and he has tweeted about this case many times—then his administration should demand an investigation by the Office of Inspector General into how this plea deal was made. The IG should also look into what actually happened in Congress.

This plea-deal agreement is a brazen attempt to cover up the noxious view of the swamp this case was exposing. The only way to really fix the problems that allowed this alleged spy ring to operate in the halls of Congress is to demand a nonpartisan investigation.

POSTSCRIPT

"[T]he more one is conscious of one's political bias, the more chance one has of acting politically without sacrificing one's aesthetic and intellectual integrity."

—George Orwell

While writing *Spies in Congress*, quite a few people looked at me quizzically and said they didn't think there was enough there for a book.

When they'd say this, I'd smile and say, "If you only knew." They'd shrug and the conversation would move on to something else.

It was hard not to be bothered by the reaction, because I knew that the media and Congress simply haven't told enough of this story for people to understand its importance. Still, I knew they had a point, as much of what is reported in this book is already mere journalistic background to a now covered-up scandal.

When I said this to Michael Waller, an author and foreign policy expert, he smiled as we crossed a street in Washington and said, "Yes, but you'll be throwing a wrecking ball into the narrative that 'there is nothing to see here.' The media and many politicians don't want that."

This made me think of George Orwell, the famed British author of *Nineteen Eighty-Four*. Orwell spent his writing career running into this problem and often turned to fiction to get to deeper truths he just couldn't narratively show in nonfiction; in fact, a publisher that had previously contracted me for this book wanted me to do just that.

"Make it a thriller," they said. "There just isn't enough narrative here." They had a point, but I turned them down and took the project to Post Hill Press, because the facts of this case needed to be told without the blur of fiction distorting the picture. The truth must come out.

On this topic, a critic once wrote Orwell about his book *Homage to Catalonia*, a first-person account of his participation in the Spanish Civil War, to ask why he'd put in a chapter that explained the Spanish politics of the time, the right and wrong of it, in the otherwise aesthetically pleasing narrative.

Orwell answered this question in an essay, "Why I Write," by explaining that "among other things [*Homage to Catalonia*] contains a long chapter, full of newspaper quotations and the like, defending the Trotskyists who were accused of plotting with Franco. Clearly such a chapter, which after a year or two would lose its interest for any ordinary reader, must ruin the book. A critic whom I respect read me a lecture about it. 'Why did you put in all that stuff?' he said. 'You've turned what might have been a good book into journalism.' What he said was true, but I could not have done otherwise. I happened to know, what very few people in England had been allowed to know, that innocent men were being falsely accused. If I had not been angry about that I should never have written the book."[1]

After spending a year digging into this story, I happen to know there is a lot here that Americans aren't being allowed to know. And that might not be dangerous if so much of our freedom weren't wrapped up in this narrative.

So yes, this book is a work of journalism, and it asks many questions it can't answer but can only hope to compel answers for later. But isn't that what a journalist up against the system should be doing?

ENDNOTES

Epigraph

[1] From the original preface to George Orwell's *Animal Farm*, as published in *George Orwell: Some Materials for a Bibliography* (1953) by Ian R. Willison.

Preface

[1] Informal congressional hearing in October 2017, https://www.youtube.com/watch?v=FPGfVZLzqXM.

[2] http://www.documentcloud.org/documents/4497879-IG-Briefing.html

[3] Shawn Boburg, "Federal Probe Into House Technology Worker Imran Awan Yields Intrigue, No Evidence of Espionage," *Washington Post*, 9/16/17, https://www.washingtonpost.com/investigations/federal-probe-into-house-technology-worker-imran-awan-yields-intrigue-no-evidence-of-espionage/2017/09/16/100b4170-93f2-11e7-b9bc-b2f7903bab0d_story.html?utm_term=.e2a9695d7cab.

[4] Informal congressional hearing in October 2017, https://www.youtube.com/watch?v=FPGfVZLzqXM.

[5] Frank Miniter, "The Exploding DNC IT Scandal Is As Crazy As Fiction," *Forbes*, 7/26/17, https://www.forbes.com/sites/frankminiter/2017/07/26/this-exploding-dnc-story-is-crazier-than-fiction-maybe-rep-wasserman-schultz-can-explain/#139f6bbf4414.

6   Gowen Rhoades Winograd & Silva PLLC, "Statement on the Imran Awan Case," http://gowenrhoades.com/wp-content/uploads/2017/07/20170725-Awan-PR-Statement.pdf.

Chapter 1

1   Urban Dictionary top definition of "IT Guys," http://www.urbandictionary.com/define.php?term=IT%20Guy.

2   Federal Bureau of Investigation, Joint Terrorism Task Forces, "What We Investigate," https://www.fbi.gov/investigate/terrorism/joint-terrorism-task-forces.

3   Testimony from Luke Rosiak at an informal congressional hearing on October 10, 2017, https://www.youtube.com/watch?v=FPGfVZLzqXM.

4   *Members' Congressional Handbook*, https://cha.house.gov/handbooks/members-congressional-handbook#Members-Handbook-Staff-Employee-Ceiling.

5   Informal congressional hearing on October 10, 2017, https://www.youtube.com/watch?v=FPGfVZLzqXM.

6   Rep. Louis Gohmert, "There Are Radical Islamists Who Want to Destroy Our Way of Life," House of Representatives, 3/10/17, https://www.congress.gov/congressional-record/2017/3/10/house-section/article/h2045-6.

7   Author interview with Kelsey Pietranton, a spokesperson for the FBI.

8   Committee on House Administration, May 21, 2008, https://www.gpo.gov/fdsys/pkg/CHRG-110hhrg44089/pdf/CHRG-110hhrg44089.pdf.

9   Ibid.

10   Shawn Boburg, "Federal Probe Into House Technology Worker Imran Awan Yields Intrigue, No Evidence of Espionage," *Washington Post*, 9/16/17, https://www.washingtonpost.com/investigations/federal-probe-into-house-technology-worker-imran-awan-yields-intrigue-no-evidence-of-espionage/2017/09/16/100b4170-93f2-11e7-b9bc-b2f7903bab0d_story.html?utm_term=.1f9c1cc27b4a.

11   Boburg, "Federal Probe."

12 Informal congressional hearing on October 10, 2017, https://www.youtube.com/watch?v=FPGfVZLzqXM.

13 This data was found at http://congressional-staff.insidegov.com/l/22830/Imran-Awan, but on 7/9/18 this site led to a page that said, "This site is no longer available. We are sorry for the inconvenience."

14 Informal congressional hearing on October 10, 2017, https://www.youtube.com/watch?v=FPGfVZLzqXM.

15 Ronna Romney McDaniel, "Need To Get To Bottom Of Debbie Wasserman-Schultz IT Security Threat Story," Fox News, 7/26/17, https://www.youtube.com/watch?v=ohTvfvr7tHk&feature=youtu.be&mid=89339&rid=33044660.

16 Informal congressional hearing in October 2017, https://www.youtube.com/watch?v=FPGfVZLzqXM.

17 This data was found at http://congressional-staff.insidegov.com/l/22517/Haseeb-A-Rana, but on 7/9/18 this site led to a page that said, "This site is no longer available. We are sorry for the inconvenience."

18 Luke Rosiak, "House Dems Hired a Fired McDonald's Worker As Their IT Guy," *Daily Caller*, 6/26/17, http://dailycaller.com/2017/06/26/house-dems-hired-a-fired-mcdonalds-worker-as-their-it-guy/.

19 Author interview with Kendra Arnold, general counsel for the Foundation for Accountability and Civic Trust (FACT).

20 Luke Rosiak, "House IT Aides Fear Suspects In Hill Breach Are Blackmailing Members with Their Own Data," *Daily Caller*, 5/21/17, http://dailycaller.com/2017/05/21/house-it-aides-fear-suspects-in-hill-breach-are-blackmailing-members-with-their-own-data/.

21 https://www.lankford.senate.gov/download/federal-fumbles-final-edition.

22 Alicia Powe, "Congressman Warns Dems Handed U.S. Secrets to Pakistanis," *WND*, 10/12/17, http://www.wnd.com/2017/10/congressman-warns-dems-handed-u-s-secrets-to-pakistanis/#zDk22Hm82ZP2112l.99.

23   Informal congressional hearing in October 2017, https://www.youtube.com/watch?v=FPGfVZLzqXM.

24   Ibid.

25   Shawn Boburg, "Federal Probe Into House Technology Worker Imran Awan Yields Intrigue, No Evidence of Espionage," *Washington Post*, 9/16/17, https://www.washingtonpost.com/investigations/federal-probe-into-house-technology-worker-imran-awan-yields-intrigue-no-evidence-of-espionage/2017/09/16/100b4170-93f2-11e7-b9bc-b2f7903bab0d_story.html?utm_term=.1f9c1cc27b4a.

26   Cars International bankruptcy records with the United States Bankruptcy Court, Eastern District of Virginia, http://www.documentcloud.org/documents/3889134-Car-Dealership-and-Al-Attar.html.

27   https://archives.fbi.gov/archives/baltimore/press-releases/2012/two-physicians-indicted-in-a-conspiracy-to-defraud-the-irs-by-concealing-their-income-and-filing-false-tax-returns.

28   According to Health Grades (https://www.healthgrades.com/physician/dr-ali-al-attar-xg73k), as retrieved in October 2017.

29   Philip Giraldi, "The Strange Case of Imran Awan," *American Conservative*, 8/3/17, http://www.theamericanconservative.com/articles/the-strange-case-of-imran-awan/.

30   Emily Babay, "Doctor Accused Making $800k-Plus from Health Care Fraud," *Washington Examiner*, 2/21/2011, http://www.washingtonexaminer.com/doctor-accused-making-800k-plus-from-health-care-fraud/article/110761.

31   Philip Giraldi, "The Strange Case of Imran Awan," *American Conservative*, 8/3/17, http://www.theamericanconservative.com/articles/the-strange-case-of-imran-awan/.

32   Philip Giraldi, "Paul Wolfowitz's Iran Connection," *American Conservative*, 6/5/2013, http://www.theamericanconservative.com/articles/paul-wolfowitzs-iran-connection/.

33   Jodi Wilgoren, "A Nation at War: Iraqi-Americans, Iraqis in U.S. Prepare to Return and Rebuild Homeland," *New York Times*, 4/11/2003, http://www.nytimes.com/2003/04/11/us/nation-war-iraqi-americans-iraqis-us-prepare-return-rebuild-homeland.html.

34 Copy of Nasir Khattak deposition, 4/6/11, http://www. documentcloud.org/documents/3889134-Car-Dealer-ship-and-Al-Attar.html.

35 Luke Rosiak, "Congress IT Probe Suspects Had Massive Debts, Years of Suspicious Activity," *Daily Caller*, 2/7/17, http://dai-lycaller.com/2017/02/07/congress-it-probe-suspects-had-mas-sive-debts-years-of-suspicious-activity/.

36 "18 Revelations from WikiLeaks' Hacked Clinton Emails," BBC News, 10/27/16, http://www.bbc.com/news/world-us-canada-37639370).

37 Copy of Josh Schwerin email, 3/7/15, https://wikileaks.org/ podesta-emails/emailid/31077.

38 Katie Bo Williams, "Comey: DNC Denied FBI's Requests for Access to Hacked Servers," *The Hill*, 1/10/17, http://thehill. com/policy/national-security/313555-comey-fbi-did-request-access-to-hacked-dnc-servers.

39 Ali Watkins, "The FBI Never Asked for Access to Hacked Computer Servers," BuzzFeed, 1/4/17, https://www.buzzfeed. com/alimwatkins/the-fbi-never-asked-for-access-to-hacked-computer-servers?utm_term=.dgr7wEZpE#.gi8OENZyN.

40 Evan Perez and Daniella Diaz, "FBI: DNC Rebuffed Request to Examine Computer Servers," CNN, 1/5/17, http://www.cnn. com/2017/01/05/politics/fbi-russia-hacking-dnc-crowdstrike/ index.htm.

41 "Julian Assange: Our Source Is Not the Russian Government," transcript from Sean Hannity's Fox News show on January 3, 2017, http://www.foxnews.com/transcript/2017/01/03/julian-assange-our-source-is-not-russian-government.html.

42 Informal House hearing in October 2017, https://www.you-tube.com/watch?v=FPGfVZLzqXM.

43 Luke Rosiak, "DWS IT Guy Was Banned from House After Trying to Hide Secret Server," *Daily Caller*, 9/12/17, http:// dailycaller.com/2017/09/12/exclusive-dws-it-guy-was-banned-from-house-after-trying-to-hide-secret-server/.

44 Luke Rosiak, "Becerra Tried to Block Server Admin Over Red Flags, but Logins Continued, with Muted Reaction," *Daily*

Caller, 12/11/17, http://dailycaller.com/2017/12/11/becerra-tried-to-block-server-admin-over-red-flags-but-logins-continued-with-muted-reaction/.

45   California Attorney General Xavier Becerra, National Press Club, 12/6/17, https://www.youtube.com/watch?v=h1hnmjclgnw.

46   Donna Brazile, *Hacks: The Inside Story of the Break-ins and Breakdowns That Put Donald Trump in the White House*, Hachette Books, November 2017.

47   Shawn Boburg, "Federal Probe Into House Technology Worker Imran Awan Yields Intrigue, No Evidence of Espionage," *Washington Post*, 9/16/17, https://www.washingtonpost.com/investigations/federal-probe-into-house-technology-worker-imran-awan-yields-intrigue-no-evidence-of-espionage/2017/09/16/100b4170-93f2-11e7-b9bc-b2f7903bab0d_story.html?utm_term=.1f9c1cc27b4a.

48   Copy of Democrats' letter to Reps. Tom Graves and Debbie Wasserman Schultz, 3/22/16, https://fas.org/irp/congress/2016_cr/hpsci-hac.pdf.

49   This data was found at http://congressional-staff.insidegov.com/l/34531/Sean-E-McCluskie, but on 7/9/18 this site led to a page that said, "This site is no longer available. We are sorry for the inconvenience."

50   Copy of Committee on House Administration statement on House theft investigation, 2/3/17, https://cha.house.gov/press-release/cha-statement-house-theft-investigation.

51   Luke Rosiak, "DWS IT Guy Was Banned from House After Trying to Hide Secret Server," *Daily Caller*, 9/12/17, http://dailycaller.com/2017/9/12/exclusive-dws-it-guy-was-banned-from-house-after-trying-to-hide-secret-server/.

52   Sabrina Eaton, "Ex-Aides to Marcia Fudge and Tim Ryan Are Focus of Investigation, Conspiracy Theories," Cleveland.com, 8/3/17, http://www.cleveland.com/open/index.ssf/2017/08/former_ohio_congress_members_s.html.

53   Rep. Scott Perry at an informal congressional hearing on October 10, 2017, https://www.youtube.com/watch?v=FPGfVZLzqXM.

54 Anthony Man, "Wasserman Schultz Talks About Arrested Aide Imran Awan," *Sun-Sentinel*, 8/3/17, http://www.sun-sentinel.com/news/politics/fl-reg-wasserman-schultz-discusses-imran-awan-20170802-story.html.

55 Copy of Americo Financial Life and Annuity Insurance Co. interpleader complaint vs. Abid Awan and Samina Ashraf Gilani, 4/14/17, https://www.documentcloud.org/documents/3679673-20170414-Complaint.html.

56 LegBranch.com, "Congressional Staff 1987-2014," http://www.legbranch.com/theblog/2016/6/17/how-many-congressional-staff-are-there.

57 Heather Caygle, "House to Brief Lawmakers On Shared Employees Amid Ongoing IT Probe," *Politico*, 11/7/17, https://www.politico.com/story/2017/11/07/house-lawmakers-it-probe-244662.

58 Joe Uchill, "Why the Latest Theory About the DNC Not Being Hacked Is Probably Wrong," *The Hill*, 8/14/17, http://thehill.com/policy/cybersecurity/346468-why-the-latest-theory-about-the-dnc-not-being-a-hack-is-probably-wrong.

59 Uchill, "Why the Latest Theory."

60 Patrick Lawrence, "A New Report Raises Big Questions About Last Year's DNC Hack," *The Nation*, 8/9/17. https://www.thenation.com/article/a-new-report-raises-big-questions-about-last-years-dnc-hack/.

61 Editorial, "Bernie Sanders for President," *The Nation*, 01/14/2016, https://www.thenation.com/article/bernie-sanders-for-president/.

62 "Intel Vets Challenge 'Russia Hack' Evidence," Consortiumnews.com, 7/24/17, https://consortiumnews.com/2017/07/24/intel-vets-challenge-russia-hack-evidence/.

Chapter 2

1 You can see Rep. Wasserman Schultz at the May 17, 2017, hearing on YouTube: https://www.youtube.com/watch?v=iMjNXJASkig.

2 Luke Rosiak, "Police Report Indicates Wasserman Schultz IT Aide Planted Computer for Investigators to Find," *Daily Caller*,

9/6/17, http://dailycaller.com/2017/09/06/exclusive-did-imran-want-capitol-police-to-find-wasserman-schultzs-laptop/.

3   Representative Wasserman Schultz at the May 17, 2017, hearing, YouTube: https://www.youtube.com/watch?v=iMjNXJASkig.

4   https://appropriations.house.gov/calendararchive/eventsingle. aspx?EventID=394870.

5   Anthony Mann, "Wasserman Schultz Warns Capitol Police Chief to Expect 'Consequences,'" *Sun-Sentinel*, 5/25/17, http:// www.sun-sentinel.com/news/politics/fl-reg-wasserman-schultz-police-chief-threat-20170525-story.html.

6   Shawn Boburg, "Federal Probe Into House Technology Worker Imran Awan Yields Intrigue, No Evidence of Espionage," *Washington Post*, 9/16/17, https://www.washingtonpost.com/investigations/federal-probe-into-house-technology-worker-imran-awan-yields-intrigue-no-evidence-of-espionage/2017/09/16/100b4170-93f2-11e7-b9bc-b2f7903bab0d_story.html?utm_term=.1f9c1cc27b4a.

7   Heather Caygle, "House to Brief Lawmakers On Shared Employees Amid Ongoing IT Probe," *Politico*, 11/7/17, https://www.politico.com/story/2017/11/07/house-lawmakers-it-probe-244662.

8   Osita Nwanevu, "Is There Anything to the Conservative Media Story About Debbie Wasserman Schultz's IT Staffers?" *Slate*, 8/4/17, (http://www.slate.com/blogs/the_slatest/2017/08/04/the_investigation_of_imran_awan_and_house_it_staffers_for_debbie_wasserman.html.

9   http://gowenrhoades.com/christopher-gowen/.

10   Author interview with Sharyl Attkisson.

11   Frank Miniter, "Documents Expose How the Obama Administration Plays the Media," *Forbes*, 12/8/14, https://www.forbes.com/sites/frankminiter/2014/12/08/documents-expose-how-the-obama-administration-plays-the-media/4/#732c09544eb4.

12   Author interview with Stephen Hunter.

13   Fredreka Schouten, "Colorado Rep. Ken Buck Pens Tell-All Book on Washington's 'Swamp,'" *USA Today*, 4/13/17, https://www.usatoday.com/story/news/politics/2017/04/10/colorado-

rep-ken-buck-writes-drain-the-swamp-book-republicans-washington/100298958/.

14 Catherine Treyz, "Sanders Campaign Sues DNC After Database Breach," CNN, 12/21/15.

15 Copy of Bernie Sanders's lawsuit against the DNC: https://berniesanders.com/wp-content/uploads/2015/12/Bernie2016vDNCComplaint.pdf.

16 Donna Brazile, "Inside Hillary Clinton's Secret Takeover of the DNC," *Politico*, 11/2/17, https://www.politico.com/magazine/story/2017/11/02/clinton-brazile-hacks-2016-215774.

17 Ben Norton, "Un-Democratic Party: DNC Chair Says Superdelegates Ensure Elites Don't Have to Run 'Against Grassroots Activists,'" *Salon*, 2/13/16.

18 Jennifer Epstein, "Obama's No-Money-From-Lobbyists Policy? Democratic Party Says Fuggedaboutit," Bloomberg, 7/23/15.

19 Donna Brazile, "Inside Hillary Clinton's Secret Takeover of the DNC," *Politico*, 11/2/17, https://www.politico.com/magazine/story/2017/11/02/clinton-brazile-hacks-2016-215774.

20 Tim Haines, "MSNBC's Mika Brzezinski Calls for DNC Chair to Step Down for Bias Against Sanders," *RealClearPolitics*, 5/18/16, https://www.realclearpolitics.com/video/2016/05/18/msnbcs_mika_brzezinski_calls_for_dnc_chair_to_step_down_for_bias_against_sanders.html.

21 Daniel Halper and Joe Tacopino, "Leaked Emails Show How Democrats Screwed Sanders," *New York Post*, 7/22/16, https://nypost.com/2016/07/22/leaked-emails-show-how-democrats-screwed-sanders/.

22 Chuck Ross, "Emails: Wasserman Schultz Was FURIOUS with Mika Brzezinski Over Criticism," *Daily Caller*, 7/22/16, http://dailycaller.com/2016/07/22/emails-wasserman-schultz-was-furious-with-mika-brzezinski-over-criticism/.

23 Alana Goodman and Shekhar Bhatia, "Pictured, the Democratic IT Aide Charged with Fraud In Congress 'Hacking' Scandal As Relative Says He 'Would Have Done Anything' for Money—Including Selling Data," *Daily Mail*, 8/23/17, http://www.daily-

mail.co.uk/news/article-4803884/Pictured-Dem-aide-charged-fraud-hacking-probe.html#ixzz4wuwbom9l.

24   Paul Sperry, "IT Staffers May Have Compromised Sensitive Data to Foreign Intelligence," *New York Post*, 8/19/17, https://nypost.com/2017/08/19/it-staffers-may-have-compromised-sensitive-data-to-foreign-intelligence/.

25   Alicia Powe, "Congressman warns Dems handed U.S. secrets to Pakistanis." WND, 10/12/17, http://www.wnd.com/2017/10/congressman-warns-dems-handed-u-s-secrets-to-pakistanis/.

Chapter 3

1   FBI affidavit in *United States of America v. Imran Awan*, U.S. District Court for the District of Columbia, 7/24/17, http://www.documentcloud.org/documents/3900669-Awan-Imran-Complaint-and-Affidavit.html.

2   Jason Goodman, "Andre Taggart in His Own Words," 8/29/17, https://www.youtube.com/watch?v=ECQqGbqET0Y.

3   Nicholas Fandosjuly, "Trump Fuels Intrigue Surrounding a Former I.T. Worker's Arrest," *New York Times*, 7/28/17, https://www.nytimes.com/2017/07/28/us/politics/imran-awan-debbie-wasserman-shultz-pakistan.html.

Chapter 4

1   Alana Goodman and Shekhar Bhatia, "Pictured, the Democratic IT Aide Charged with Fraud In Congress 'Hacking' Scandal As Relative Says He 'Would Have Done Anything' for Money— Including Selling Data," *Daily Mail*, 8/23/17.

2   Nicholas Fandos, "Trump Fuels Intrigue Surrounding a Former I.T. Worker's Arrest," *New York Times*, 7/28/17, https://www.nytimes.com/2017/07/28/us/politics/imran-awan-debbie-wasserman-shultz-pakistan.html.

3   Author interview with George Webb.

4   Copy of police Calls for Service Report filed by Sumaira Siddique, 7/18/16, http://www.documentcloud.org/documents/4053521-CFS-E16-2002408-R-Siddiqui.html.

5   Abid Khan, "Wife of Pakistan-American IT Consultant Complains of Fraud," ARY News, 9/29/17, https://arynews.tv/en/wife-of-pakistan-american-it-consultant-complains-of-fraud/.

6   Copy of police Incident/Investigation Report report filed by Salam Chaudry, 9/11/17, http://www.documentcloud.org/documents/4053520-CASE-20153610202-R-Chaudry.html.

7   Copy of police Incident/Investigation Report filed by Samina Gilani, 1/5/17, http://www.documentcloud.org/documents/3516620-Abid-Awan-s-stepmother-calls-the-police-on-the.html.

8   Virginia State Bar Disciplinary Board, Order of Suspension for Michael Mitry Hadeed Jr., 9/30/10, http://www.vsb.org/docs/Hadeed-102210.pdf.

9   US District Court for the District of Columbia, Consent to Quash Warrant and Issue Criminal Summons, 9/6/17, https://www.docdroid.net/CJZ9fym/23-main.pdf.

10 Luke Rosiak, "Wasserman Schultz IT Aide Allegedly Bragged He Paid Pakistani Police for Protection," *Daily Caller*, 10/2/17, http://dailycaller.com/2017/10/02/wasserman-schultz-it-aide-bragged-he-paid-pakistani-police-for-protection/.

11 Stephen Dinan, "Judge Orders Feds to Help Two More 17-Year-Old Illegal Immigrant Girls Get Abortions," *Washington Times*, 12/18/17, https://www.washingtontimes.com/news/2017/dec/18/Tanya-chutkan-feds-must-help-illegals-get-abortion/.

12 "JoAnna Wasserman, Michael Marando," *New York Times*, 4/26/2015, https://www.nytimes.com/2015/04/26/fashion/weddings/26WassermanMarando.html.

13 Steven Wasserman, Twitter tweets from August 1017, https://twitter.com/fedpros/status/893932147156946945.

Chapter 5

1   Crowdsource the Truth video: https://www.youtube.com/watch?v=ECQqGbqET0Y.

2   Frank Miniter, "The Exploding DNC IT Scandal Is As Crazy As Fiction," *Forbes,* July 26, 2017, https://www.forbes.com/sites/frankminiter/2017/07/26/this-exploding-dnc-story-is-crazier-than-fiction-maybe-rep-wasserman-schultz-can-explain/#139f6bbf4414.

3   Anthony Man, "Wasserman Schultz Talks About Arrested Aide Imran Awan," *Sun-Sentinel,* 8/3/17, http://www.sun-sentinel.com/news/politics/fl-reg-wasserman-schultz-discusses-imran-awan-20170802-story.html.

4   Nicholas Fandos, "Trump Fuels Intrigue Surrounding a Former I.T. Worker's Arrest," *New York Times,* 7/28/17, https://www.nytimes.com/2017/07/28/us/politics/imran-awan-debbie-wasserman-shultz-pakistan.html.

5   Crowdsource the Truth video: https://www.youtube.com/watch?v=ECQqGbqET0Y.

6   Copy of Jesse Winograd, letter to Mr. and Mrs. Andre Taggart, 9/1/17, http://www.documentcloud.org/documents/4390229-20170901-Letter.html.

7   MSNBC's "Morning Joe," http://www.msnbc.com/morning-joe/watch/rep-becerra-trump-is-a-bigoted-man-710371395630, 6/22/16.

8   Heather Caygle, "House Democrats Fire Two IT Staffers Amid Criminal Investigation," *Politico,* 3/1/17, https://www.politico.com/story/2017/03/house-democrats-it-staffers-hina-alvi-imran-awan-235569.

9   Jana Winter, "Some Muslims Attending Capitol Hill Prayer Group Have Terror Ties, Probe Reveals," Fox News, 11/11/2010, http://www.foxnews.com/politics/2010/11/11/congressional-muslim-prayer-group-terror-ties.html.

10   The embassy of Pakistan scrubbed a link to this conference: http://www.embassyofpakistanusa.org/news97.php.

11   Terrence McCoy, "Fourteen Years Ago, He Was a Convicted Jihadist. Now He's Fighting Radical Islam Steps from The White House," *Washington Post,* 7/7/2017, https://www.washingtonpost.com/local/social-issues/fourteen-years-ago-he-was-convicted-jihadist-now-hes-fighting-radical-islam-steps-from-the-white-

house/2017/07/07/019a7b18-47aa-11e7-98cd-af64b4fe2dfc_story.html?utm_term=.2f6fe0d0e66c.

12   Isabel Vincent and Melissa Klein, "Rep. Meeks helped 'jihad' flier," *New York Post*, 9/20/10, https://www.investigativeproject.org/2190/rep-meeks-helped-jihad-flier.

Chapter 6

1   Author interview with Clare Lopez, vice president for research and analysis for the Center for Security Policy.

2   "Influential expat shields father from long arm of law," Dawn, 9/4/2009, https://www.dawn.com/news/944935/influential-expat-shields-father-from-long-arm-of-law.

3   Author interview with Lawrence Sellin.

4   Shamil Shams, "A Look at Complex CIA-ISI Ties Through Raymond Davis Saga," DW, 3/7/2017, http://www.dw.com/en/a-look-at-complex-cia-isi-ties-through-raymond-davis-saga/a-39521883.

5   Asad Kharal, "After Davis' arrest, US operatives leaving Pakistan," The Express Tribune, 2/28/2011, https://tribune.com.pk/story/124965/intelligence-assets-after-davis-arrest-us-operatives-leaving-pakistan/.

6   Mark Mazzetti, Eric Schmitt, and Charlie Savage, "Pakistan Spies on Its Diaspora, Spreading Fear," *New York Times*, 7/23/2011, http://www.nytimes.com/2011/07/24/world/asia/24isi.html?hpw=&pagewanted=all.

7   Mazzetti, Schmitt, and Savage, "Pakistan Spies on Its Diaspora."

8   Luke Rosiak and Wajid Ali Syed, "'Pakistani Mystery Man': Awans' Father Transferred Data To Pakistani Government, Ex-Partner Claims," *Daily Caller*, 4/18/2018. (http://dailycaller.com/2018/04/18/imran-awan-usb-drive-pakistan/)

9   Shawn Boburg, "Federal Probe Into House Technology Worker Imran Awan Yields Intrigue, No Evidence of Espionage," *Washington Post*, 9/16/17, https://www.washingtonpost.com/investigations/federal-probe-into-house-technology-worker-imran-awan-yields-

intrigue-no-evidence-of-espionage/2017/09/16/100b4170-93f2-11e7-b9bc-b2f7903bab0d_story.html?utm_term=.1f9c1cc27b4a.

10   Kenneth P. Vogel, "'Isn't That the Trump Lawyer?': A Reporter's Accidental Scoop," *New York Times*, 9/17/17, https://www.nytimes.com/2017/09/19/us/politics/isnt-that-the-trump-lawyer-a-reporters-accidental-scoop.html.

11   Informal congressional hearing in October 2017, https://www.youtube.com/watch?v=FPGfVZLzqXM.

12   Alicia Powe, "Congressman Warns Dems Handed U.S. Secrets to Pakistanis," *WND*, 10/12/17, http://mobile.wnd.com/2017/10/congressman-warns-dems-handed-u-s-secrets-to-pakistanis/.

13   Luke Rosiak, "Wasserman Schultz IT Aide Allegedly Bragged He Paid Pakistani Police for Protection," *Daily Caller*, 10/2/17, http://dailycaller.com/2017/10/02/wasserman-schultz-it-aide-bragged-he-paid-pakistani-police-for-protection/.

14   Nate Lord, "An Expert Guide to Securing Sensitive Data: 34 Experts Reveal the Biggest Mistakes Companies Make with Data Security," *Data Insider*, 2/16/2018, https://digitalguardian.com/blog/expert-guide-securing-sensitive-data-34-experts-reveal-biggest-mistakes-companies-make-data.

15   Informal House hearing in October 2017, https://www.youtube.com/watch?v=FPGfVZLzqXM.

16   Alana Goodman and Shekhar Bhatia, "Pictured, the Democratic IT Aide Charged with Fraud In Congress 'Hacking' Scandal As Relative Says He 'Would Have Done Anything' for Money—Including Selling Data," *Daily Mail*, 8/23/17.

17   Shawn Boburg, "Federal Probe Into House Technology Worker Imran Awan Yields Intrigue, No Evidence of Espionage," *Washington Post*, 9/16/17, https://www.washingtonpost.com/investigations/federal-probe-into-house-technology-worker-imran-awan-yields-intrigue-no-evidence-of-espionage/2017/09/16/100b4170-93f2-11e7-b9bc-b2f7903bab0d_story.html?utm_term=.1f9c1cc27b4a.

18   Copy of Nasir Khattak deposition, 4/6/11, http://www.documentcloud.org/documents/3889134-Car-Dealership-and-Al-Attar.html.

19   Pinterest.com, photo of hairstyle model, https://www.google.com/imgres?imgurl=https://i.pinimg.com/736x/65/e0/5f/65e05f363ca3f0e1cdd67679e2cba404--mohawk-hairstyles-hairstyles-for-short-hair.jpg&imgrefurl=https://www.pinterest.com/kristsuarez/mens-hair-styles/&h=400&w=286&tbnid=k1F59TvGRzqXWM&tbnh=266&tbnw=190&usg=__RwcxmHMPHekndM7zQBPdbpga3rk=&hl=en&docid=ivkAp5CbwSra7M&itg=1.

20   BizStanding.com, Alain LLC company profile, https://bizstanding.com/p/alain+llc-155675273.

21   Copy of Imran Awan affidavit filed in Fairfax General District Court, 10/18/16, https://www.documentcloud.org/documents/3983049-Scan.html.

Chapter 7

1   Sen. Rand Paul (R-KY) in an interview on Fox News' "FOX & Friends," 6/6/17, http://insider.foxnews.com/2017/06/06/rand-paul-i-guarantee-unmaskers-left-paper-trail.

2   Author interview with Tom Fitton, president of Judicial Watch.

3   US House of Representatives Committee on Rules, "Laws That Do Not Apply To Congress," https://archives-democrats-rules.house.gov/archives/jcoc2ai.htm.

4   Informal congressional hearing in October 2017, https://www.youtube.com/watch?v=FPGfVZLzqXM.

5   US House of Representatives: History, Art and Archives, Congressional Oath of Office, http://history.house.gov/Institution/Origins-Development/Oath-of-Office/.

6   Maria Abi-Habib, Facebook post, 7/21/16, https://www.facebook.com/maria.abihabib/posts/10153973225688533.

7   US Customs and Border Protection, "CBP Releases Statistics on Electronic Device Searches," 4/11/17, https://www.cbp.gov/newsroom/national-media-release/cbp-releases-statistics-electronic-device-searches-0.

8   Author interview with Adam Schwartz, senior staff attorney for the Electronic Frontier Foundation.

9   Author interview with Brad Serwin, general counsel at Glassdoor.

10   https://assets.documentcloud.org/documents/3939670/8-22-17-US-Reply-Brief-DreamHost.pdf.

11   DreamHost.com, "A Win for Privacy Is a Win for the Web," https://www.dreamhost.com/blog/a-win-for-the-web/.

12   US Department of Justice, "Government's reply in support of its motion to show cause, and motion to modify Attachment B of the search warrant," August 2017, https://www.scribd.com/document/356964456/DreamHost-Government-Reply-August-2017.

Chapter 8

1   FBI affidavit of Imran Awan: https://www.documentcloud.org/documents/3900669-Awan-Imran-Complaint-and-Affidavit.html

Postscript

1   George Orwell, "Why I Write," essay, 1946.

ACKNOWLEDGMENTS

It is a delicate thing to thank anonymous sources, as readers are understandably suspicious of those who want their names kept out of print. But without them this book would have only been an outsider's perspective. Anonymous sources, in this case, were critical to finding the truth, because they gave specifics rooted in personal experience about the villains of this tale. They also gave important background on how the US House of Representatives actually functions. Many did so knowing if they were found out, their careers on Capitol Hill would be in jeopardy. So all of you—and you know who you are— please accept my heartiest thank-you.

Many others could be quoted and named openly in this book. Still, they didn't have to take the time to give their perspectives, but they did. This is also no small thing, as even much of the Republican leadership and the Republican National Committee declined to be interviewed for this spy story and criminal investigation involving dozens of members of Congress, all Democrats.

ABOUT THE AUTHOR

Frank Miniter is an investigative journalist and the author of *The Ultimate Man's Survival Guide: Recovering the Lost Art of Manhood.* He is also the author of *Kill Big Brother*, a cyber thriller on how we can keep our freedom in this age of terror, as well as *This Will Make a Man of You: One Man's Search for Hemingway and Manhood in a Changing World, Saving the Bill of Rights*, and *The Future of the Gun.* Miniter writes for Fox News and numerous publications including *Americas 1*st *Freedom.*